THE CHRISTIAN WALK: THE STRUGGLE TO REMAIN ON THE PATH

by

Dr. Sheila Carpenter

eShore

Pittsburgh, PA

ISBN 1-58501-036-7

Trade Paperback
© Copyright 2002 Dr. Sheila Carpenter
All Rights Reserved
First Printing — 2002
Second Printing — 2002
Library of Congress #2001094817

Request for information should be addressed to:

SterlingHouse Publisher, Inc.
7436 Washington Avenue
Suite 200
Pittsburgh, PA 15218
www.sterlinghousepublisher.com

CeShore is an imprint of SterlingHouse Publisher, Inc.
Cover Design: Jeffrey S. Butler — SterlingHouse Publisher, Inc.
Book Design: Kathleen M. Gall

This publication includes images from Corel Draw 8 which are protected
by the copyright laws of the U.S., Canada, and elsewhere.

Printed in the United States of America

PREFACE

No one can understand how serious it was for me to write this book. Christians live in and deal with a world that the devil has control of, but all of the power rests within God!

Sometimes we, as Christians, ask ourselves the question, "God, where are you? Don't you see the world in a hectic state, children killing children, the elderly getting beaten down. How do Christians survive in a world like this? Are we not praying enough, fasting enough, or are we lacking in our faith?"

After researching and writing on this topic, I have come to a better understanding of how to function in a dysfunctional society.

ACKNOWLEDGMENTS

I give all thanks and praise to God, my Father, Jesus Christ my Personal Savior and the Holy Spirit who dwells inside of me. Because without them I could not have accomplished this goal.

I would like to thank Thomas E. Friskney for all his teachings, Moody Bible Press for letting me use some of their works and, Cincinnati Bible College for all their support; and my church family the Temple Baptist Church of Cleveland, Ohio. And, last but not least, La Salle University for giving me the opportunity to be in their Doctorate Program of Theocentric Psychology.

DEDICATION

This book is dedicated to:

FOREST W. CARPENTER

JOYCE J. GRAYS

VERA L. JACKSON

KIM, STELLA, GLYNDA, ROBERT

TEMPLE BAPTIST CHURCH

THOMAS E. FRISKNEY

TINA R. HALL

DR. A. E. CAMPBELL, JR.

PASTOR JOHN JACKSON CAMPBELL

TABLE OF CONTENTS

WHAT
IS A
CHRISTIAN?

In order to understand how a Christian can function in a dysfunctional society, the question must be asked, what is a Christian? Sometimes individuals, in society as a whole, misconceive the meaning of the word Christian. Some people feel that being good, sweet, and kind makes them Christians. Others might feel that going to church services on Christmas, Thanksgiving, Easter, or any other holiday makes them true Christians. Some might say, "Well, church is in your heart; so I really don't need to go to church. I'll read my Bible occasionally and watch some television evangelist on Sunday." Does this make them true Christians? Society says that doing good deeds, such as helping the homeless, feeding the hungry, and clothing those who do not have any clothes makes them Christians.

Dr. Spiras Zodhiates is a Twentieth Century Biblical Scholar who has interpreted and explained the Bible in its whole entirety in the Hebrew-Greek language. He is a recognized authority on the Greek New Testament and has edited a edition of the Modern Greek New Testament, which was published by the Million Testaments Campaigns and the American Bible Society. Dr. Zodhiates gives us the Greek definition of the word *Christian* in the New Testament Hebrew-Greek Key Study Bible. Dr. Zodhiates describes a *Christian* as a follower of Jesus Christ. The Greek word *Christianos* asserts this definition: "Then said

Jesus unto his disciples, if any man will come after me, let him deny himself, and take up his cross, and follow me." (Matt. 16:24) Kurt F. Reinhardt, a Twentieth Century Professor of Emeritus Theology, and the author of *The Agony of Christianity,* says, "The true Christian makes himself another Christ."

Given these definitions, we must still apply it to our original question—how does a person becomes a Christian? What comes first?

The Bible says in order for a person to *become* a Christian: 1) They must believe that Jesus Christ is the Son of the Living God. John 3:16 says, "For God so loved the world that He gave His only begotten Son, that whosoever believeth in Him should not perish, but have everlasting life." The key word here is *believeth,* to commit to trust in the Lord. 2) A person must also acknowledge the Lord Jesus Christ. "That if thou shalt confess with thy mouth the Lord Jesus, and shalt believe in thine heart that God hath risen him from the dead, thou shalt be saved." (Rom. 10:9) Again we see the word *believe* which reinforces the acknowledgment of Christ. 3) Repentance is the third step, and repentance means to think differently and give up your old ways for new ones. "Then Peter said unto them, 'Repent and be baptized every one of you in the name of Jesus Christ for the remission of sins and ye shall receive the gift of the Holy Ghost'" (Acts 2:38). When a person goes through these three steps *(Belief, Acknowledgment, and Repentance)* he is a Christian. Baptism is the fourth step. Baptism by water is an outward sign of obedience, showing fellow brothers and sisters in Christ that your old ways have been given up for a new life in Christ Jesus. "He that believeth and is baptized shall be saved; but he that believeth not shall be damned." (Mark 16:16) Here, again, the word *believe* is mentioned, which is a vital key in becoming saved. One must recognize, however, that there is more to being a Christian than these four steps.

FOOTNOTES:

Matt. 10:32

Whosoever therefore shall confess me before men, him will I confess also before my Father which is in heaven.

Luke 12:8

Also I say unto you, whosoever shall confess me before men, him shall the Son of man also confess before the angels of God.

The Lord wants more from his followers, and a Christian must try to accomplish Christ's every step. Studying is one of the most essential parts of being a Christian. Studying brings a Christian closer to God because it enhances a Christian's education, comprehension and discernment. By education a Christian's knowledge and skills can be enhanced. Their comprehension increases because their education and discernment solidify by intertwining all three in one. The Bible says, "Study to show thyself approved unto God, a workman that needeth not to be ashamed, rightly dividing the word of truth." (2 Tim. :15) Timothy explains in this passage of scripture that Christians must decipher the difference between false teachers and misrepresentations of the Word of God. If a Christian doesn't study the Word of God, society can make any interpretation they want. This is why it is very crucial for a Christian to study God's Holy Word.

For example, when individuals join a group or club, they attempt to study all the rules and regulations and know what the organization has to offer. Whenever individuals want to join an organization, they must be able to tell leaders what they expect from that organization. Jesus makes this same point with his followers: Know him and his Father, and know that the foundation of Christianity is guided by his Father, the Holy Spirit and himself.

Anyone who scrutinizes the Holy Bible has the cognizance that Jesus Christ is the Son of the Living God. The big question here is, though, how can God be three in one: God the Father, Son and the Holy Ghost. Here is a brief illustration.

An egg has three parts. The shell is a representation of God the Father. "In the beginning, God created the Heavens and the Earth." (Gen. 1:1) "And God said, 'Let us make man in our image, after our likeness.'" (Gen. 1:26) Now, the word us is plural, not singular. "In the beginning was the Word, and the Word was with God and the Word was God." (John 1:1) "And the Word was made flesh, and dwelt among us. And we behold His glory, the glory of the only begotten of the Father, full of grace and truth." (John 1:14)

The yolk of the egg, the second part of the illustration, represents Jesus Christ as the second entity. "For God so loved the world, that he gave his only begotten Son, that whosoever believeth in him should not perish, but have everlasting life." (John 3:16) "For God sent not his Son into the world to condemn the world; but that the world through him might be saved." (John 3:17) "He that believeth on him is not condemned: but he that believeth not is condemned already, because he hath not believed in the name of the only begotten Son of God." (John 3:18) The remainder of the egg, the albumen—the clear part around the yolk—is the Holy Ghost. "But the Comforter, which is the Holy Ghost, whom the Father will send in My name, shall teach you all things, and bring all things to your remembrance, whatsoever I have said unto you." (John 14:26)

This brief illustration of the egg gives the

overview of how God can be three in one, and, for a person to perceive what a Christian really is, they must comprehend this foundation of Christianity. The illustration supports the concept of the belief, acknowledgment, and repentance steps in becoming a Christian: believing God is the Creator, he sent his Son to save the world; the Holy Ghost is the Comforter to show and give gifts; and acknowledging that they are three in one. Repenting—knowing that your old ways are not Godly and that you need God, Jesus, and the Holy Spirit in order to be on the right track.

The Christian creed helps Christians become steadfast on what they believe after having been saved. The Creed states:

I believe in God the Father Almighty, and in Jesus Christ, His only begotten Son, our Lord who was born of the Holy Ghost and Virgin Mary, and was crucified under Pontius Pilate, and was buried; and the third day rose again from the dead. Ascended into heaven, sitteth on the right hand of the Father; whence he shall come to judge the quick and the dead; and in the Holy Ghost; the Holy Church; the remission of sin; and the resurrection of the flesh, Amen.

A person can memorize this creed by heart, but, if they don't practice what they preach, then it's all in vain.

Another example of the Creed is that Jesus is

"the man for others," the one in whom love completely rules, the one who is open to, and united with, the ground of his being. And this "life for others, through participation in the Being of God," is transcendence, for, at the point of love "to the uttermost," we encounter God, the ultimate depth of our being, the unconditional in the conditioned. This is what the New Testament means by saying that "God was in Christ" and "What God was, the Word was." Because Christ was utterly and completely "the man for others," because he was love. He was personified "one with the Father" because 'God is Love.' For this very reason he was the son of man, the servant of the Lord. He was indeed "one of us ..." The life of God, the ultimate Word of Love in which all things cohere, is ever completely, unconditionally, and without reserve in the life of a man—the man for others and the man of God. He is perfect man and perfect God—not as a mixture of oil and water, natural and supernatural—but as the embodiment through obedience of "the beyond in our midst," of the transcendence of love. (J.A.T. Robinson, *Honest to God*, p. 76)

Jesus tells us in Matthew 28:19-20, "Go ye therefore and teach all nations baptizing them in the name of the Father, Son and of the Holy Ghost, teaching Christians to observe all things whatsoever I have commanded you, and lo, I will be with you always, even until the end of the world. Amen." Being a Christian one must be able to equip themselves to spread the Word of God. This is a commandment of Jesus Christ, so others can follow the path. Being a Christian is very difficult at times, but there is one idea Christians want to convey to others; that if you focus on Jesus Christ, there is nothing you cannot conquer or accomplish. The Bible says, "I can do all things through Christ which strengthen me" (Phil. 4:13). "Let your light so shine before men, that they may see your good works, so they may know and glorify your Father which is in Heaven." (Matt. 5:16)

These are some commands on which a Christian must stand firm:

1) Must gird up the loins of your mind. Take a stand, face the trials that one must go through. (1 Pet. 1:13)

2) A Christian must be sober. The Greek word here is *nepho:* to live soberly and righteously (1 Pet. 1:13) (Other scripture references for these commands: 1 Thess. 5:6; Titus 2:11-12).

3) Hope to the end for the grace that is to be brought unto you at the revelation of Jesus Christ. (1 Pet. 1:13)

4) As obedient children, not fashioning your-selves according to the former lusts in your ignorance. (1 Pet. 1:14) Do not pattern after

your former life of sin. (Eph. 2:1-3). In God you are a new creature so we must walk in our new life. (1 Cor. 5:17-18)

5) Be ye holy in all your manner of life (1 Pet. 1:15-16)

6) A Christian must pattern after God in all things. "Be ye holy; for I am holy" (1 Pet. 1:16)

7) Pass the time of your sojourning here in fear: (1 Pet. 1:17).

8) Seeing ye have purified your souls in obeying the truth through the Spirit unto unfeigned love of the brethren see that ye love one another with a pure heart fervently. (1 Pet. 1:22)

The substratum of Christianity is based on the death, burial, and resurrection of Jesus Christ; also in these illustrations, faith in believing, acknowledgment, and repentance. These authors let us know that without these steps one cannot be a true Christian.

When a Christian submits himself to walk like Christ there are some guidelines he must follow:

1) A Christian must be ye all of one mind (1 Pet. 3:8)

2) Have compassion one for another. (1 Pet. 3:8)

3) Love your brethren (1 Pet. 3:8)

4) Be pitiful (1 Pet. 3:8)

5) Be courteous (1 Pet. 3:8)

6) Not rendering evil for evil (1 Pet. 3:9)

7) Nor labeling for labeling. (1 Pet. 3:9)

8) Be a blessing to others (1 Pet. 3:9)

9) Control the tongue (1 Pet. 3:10)

The Apostle Paul tells us this in II Corinthians 4:8-11, "We are troubled on every side, yet not distressed; we are perplexed, but not in despair; persecuted, but not forsaken; cast down, but not destroyed; always bearing about in the body the dying of the Lord Jesus, that the life also of Jesus might be made manifest in our body." This scripture explains to us that obstacles are going to come and we should be prepared for the unexpected. A Christian must understand that by walking in Christ people must deny themselves and take up the cross and follow Jesus, and that means give up all your worldly possessions to fight temptation and let Jesus lead. When Satan knows that Jesus leads, he will make your life troubled in every way, and that's why the Apostle Paul states, "Let Jesus be made manifest in your life so you can overcome any obstacle in your path, that Satan tries to throw out." Jesus being present in life is one of the many blessings of being a Christian.

Karl Karistsky a Twentieth Century Bible Scholar, the author of *Foundation of Christianity,* says, "There is no religion without contradictions.

None of them arose in a single mind by a purely logical process, each one is the product of manifold social influences, often going back centuries and reflecting very diverse historical situation."

Karl Karistsky's words, there is no religion without contradictions, are accurate, because in every man's theology man always tries to justify society's needs by their own actions. In Christianity, however, there is no defiance because Christ is the overseer of Christianity.

More than any other religion, Christianity relies highly on the acceptance of an historical improbability, namely, that one particular man was no mere mortal, but 'the Christ,' whose death changed the course of human history forever and who continues to exist as "God the Son," part of an indivisible, threefold Godhead. (Kreeft, Peter. *Is Christianity True?*, p. 3) Christ in the Christian, the Christian in Christ. The worshiper is incorporated into Christ, into the sacrifice; he becomes one with it as he becomes one with food, since in the Eucharist, which is the Christian sacrament commemorating Christ's Last Supper. Communion, Christ's sacrifice, is assimilated as food—you are what you eat. In the Eucharist, Christ and Christian became one. The mystery defies words; only *in* will do. Christ, by his *in*-carnation incorporated or (*in*-bodied) humanity *in*to his divinity, so that when we are *in*-

corporated into His body, his divinity is incorporated into our humanity." (Kreeft, Peter. *Making Sense out of Suffering*, p. 17)

Being a Christian has its advantages. People can talk to God twenty-four hours a day, seven days a week. Nobody is put on hold, and he will listen to every word that is said. "For the eyes of the Lord are over the righteous, and his eyes are open unto their prayers: but the face of the Lord is against them that do evil." (1 Pet. 3:12)

One question has been answered: the meaning of a Christian. The other one hasn't. What is a dysfunctional society? There are many thoughts as to what is dysfunctional: our political part of society; the government, such as today's Presidential White House scandals; to police brutality; to today's society practicing many different anti-Christian pagan religions. Dysfunctional is the opposite of functional which means to connect properly. Therefore, when a Christian works with someone or something dysfunctional it is not connected properly.

What is a dysfunctional society? In my opinion a dysfunctional society is one in which the vast majority does not link together as one. For example, in the book of Romans beginning with the 24th verse in the first chapter, the Apostle Paul tells us how dysfunctional the Roman society was in not communicating or linking

14

with God. They were making animals to be gods, immoral sexual conduct was prevalent, and sinning was rampant. To the dysfunctional society nothing was improper because all the activities they were indulging in, to them, were proper. The Apostle Paul warns that wrath results when God's grace is rejected. Romans 1:32 says, "Who knowing the judgment of God, that they which commit such things are worthy of death, not only do the same, but have pleasure in them that do them." The Romans sinned so badly that they enjoyed these sins and were encouraging others to sin also. The dysfunction is that God wasn't the Lord of their lives.

So how can a Christian walk a straight path in a dysfunctional society? Christians can only function in a dysfunctional society when God is the head of their lives. "But seek ye first the kingdom of God, and His righteousness, and all these things shall be added unto you." (Matt. 6:33) "The Lord is my light and my salvation; whom shall I fear? The Lord is the strength of my life; of whom shall I be afraid?" (Ps. 27:1) "The Lord will give strength unto His people; the Lord will bless His people with peace." (Ps. 29:11) When a Christian seeks, and asks for, strength from the Lord, God's grace prevails over all dysfunctional situations.

PRAYER, FASTING AND FAITH: WHAT THESE WONDERS CAN REALLY ACCOMPLISH

Prayer is another tool a Christian can use to function in a dysfunctional society. "The effectual fervent prayer of a righteous man answereth much." (James 5:16) Even though prayer is important, one must also have the faith within the prayer, because without faith prayer is irrelevant. "Now faith is the substance of things hoped for, the evidence of things not seen." (Heb. 11:1) Faith gives the reality of things hoped for to the things not seen. While a Christian lives in a society where situations are dysfunctional, faith assures that things will get much better.

Prayer. How can one define prayer? It can be defined as "an uplifting of the soul to God." Prayer can also be defined as "an act of love and adoration towards Him from whom comes the wonder which is life." In fact, prayer represents man's effort to communicate with an invisible being, creator of all that exists, the holder of supreme wisdom, strength, and beauty, and the Father and Savior of each one of us. Far from consisting in a simple recitation of formulas, true prayer represents a mystic state when the consciousness is absorbed in God. This state is not of an intellectual nature; it remains as inaccessible, as incomprehensible, to the philosophers and to the learned. Just as with the sense of beauty and of love, it requires no book knowledge. The simple are conscious of God as naturally as of the warmth of the sun or the perfume of a flower, but this God, so approachable by those who know how to love, is hidden from those who know only how to understand. Thought and word are at fault when it is a matter of describing this state. "That is why prayer finds its highest expression in a soaring of love through the obscure night of the intelligence." That is the theosophical psychology that Dr. Alexis Carrel described prayer as being. Dr. Carrell (1873-1944) was a twentieth century theologian and biologist who discovered a method of suturing blood vessels which made it possible to replace arteries. He was awarded the 1912 Nobel Prize for physiological medicine.

Other philosophers follow what Martin Luther says about prayer. "Prayer and nothing but prayer." In other words, "He who does not pray or call upon God in his hour of need, assuredly does not think of Him as God, nor does he give Him the honor that is His due." *(Good History and Historians,* edited by C. T. McIntire)

The great evangelical mystic, Johann Arndt, constantly emphasizes the truth that "Without prayer we cannot find God; prayer is the means by which we seek and find Him." Schleiermacher, the restorer of evangelical theology in the nineteenth century observed: "To be religious is what thinking is to philosophy." Praying is religion in the making. The religious philosopher Gustan Theordor Fechner who lived in the nineteenth century, impressively stated, "Take prayer out of the world and it is if you had torn asunder the tie that binds humanity to God, and had struck dumb the tongue of the child in the presence of his Father." *(Good History and Historians,* edited by C. T. McIntire)

Prayer is, therefore, a living communion of the religious man with God, a communion which reflects the forms of the sound relations of humanity.

There is another way of describing prayer, however. The nearest thing is poise; *P-O-I-S-E,* in thinking, in understanding, in one's outlook on life, in praying. Praying really is important above all else. Is it rarest in it's scarcity? Certainly it is rarest in its preciousness, its value. Prayer is the master key to all else. Prayer is the door, and it opens the way to living a true, human life. Prayer leads to the solutions of every baffling problem, the answer to every teasing, perplexing question, the realization of every natural longing. So it helps to clarify one's thinking as to just what prayer really is. For have some of us had rather hazy ideas about what prayer really is?

Prayer is not overcoming God's reluctance. It is taking hold of God's eager willingness. It isn't a matter of being earnest enough and pleading with intense longing for long enough until God listens and consents to do what is asked. Prayer is giving Jesus an open door down to earth. Through human consent he enters anew into human life and, so, does what he is so eager to do.

Bible study is seeing things on earth through God's eyes, and in the Bible God talks with us. God talks to the readers through the whole book from the first of Genesis to the finish of John's Revelation. The Bible is another guide to answered prayer!

In the story part, the incidents, the love stories and the tragedies, the rhythmic sobs and songs of David, the tense prophetic pleading; in and through all, in between the lines, one comes face to face with God; his love, his patience. It is constantly enforced with a human stubbornness, in the face of love's pleadings.

Here's an example of a love story. David and Bathsheba. David was in love with a married woman. He lusted after her. He murdered her husband Uriah deliberately to get to Bathsheba. As stated earlier, one comes face to face with God. "And when the mourning was past, David sent and fetched her to his house, and she became his wife, and bore him a son. But the thing that David had done displeased the Lord." (2 Sam. 11:27) "Wherefore hast thou despised the commandment of the Lord, to do evil in his sight? Thou has killed Uriah the Hittite with the sword, and has taken has wife to be thou wife, and hast slain him with the sword of the children of Ammon. Now therefore, the sword shall never depart from thine house, because thou hast despised me, and hast taken the wife of Uriah the Hittite to be thy wife. Thus saith the lord, "Behold, I will raise up evil against thee out of thine own house, and I will take thy wives before thine eyes, and give them unto thy neighbour, and he shall lie with thy wives in the sight of this sun." (2 Sam. 12:9-11) And, so, as one quietly absorbs the book, its atmosphere, its God looking eagerly out of every page, the man, himself, changes. And so it is a changed man praying. And it is a changed prayer. It becomes simple, sure, really intelligent, poised praying. Things that need changing, do change.

Let us read more thoughtfully, then we will pray more intelligently, expectantly, and persistently. This will help our Lord Jesus in his plan for things on earth. These are the beautiful words of S.D. Gordon, *Prayer and The Bible.*

Prayer, fasting and faith actually solidify a person's intimate relationship with Jesus Christ, and one can really obtain a relationship by communication. Communication actually raises the level of the relationship through prayer; through telling God how one feels and about what's going on around them. If a person doesn't know how to pray and communicate with God, Jesus gives us a Motto Prayer to show us how to communicate with God, the prayer in Matthew

6:9-13. This prayer is for Christians who don't know how to make their request be known unto God. By this prayer, a beginner can interpret what should be said and asked for. We must ask the question, what is this prayer really expressing? What is this prayer really saying when one says:

Our Father which art in heaven

The prayer acknowledges God for being in heaven, ruling, to help us to believe, this day, that there is a power to lift us up which is stronger than all the things that hold us down.

Hallowed by Thy name

Help us to be sensitive to what is beautiful, and responsive enough to what is good, so that day-by-day we may grow more sure of life's holiness, in which we want to trust.

Thy kingdom come

Help us to be quick and ready to encourage whatever brings the better meaning of God into that which otherwise might be the common ground of the uninspired day.

Thy will be done, on earth as it is in heaven.

Help us to believe that the ideals of the spirit

aren't a far-off dream, but a power to command our loyalty and direct our life here on earth.

Give us this day our daily bread.

Lord, thank you for this day, and give us the necessities we would need to withhold the day's events. Open the way for us to earn an honest living without anxiety; but let us never forget the needs of others.

And forgive us our debts, as we forgive our debtors.

Lord make us patient and sympathetic with the shortcomings of others, especially of those we love. Keep us sternly watchful only of our own. Let us never grow hard with the unconscious cruelty of those who measure themselves by mean standards, and so think they have excelled. Keep our eyes lifted to the highest, so that we may be humbled. We should see failures of others and be forgiving, because we know how much there is of which we, also, need to be forgiven.

And lead us not into temptation but deliver us from evil.

Lord let us not go carelessly this day within the reach of any evil we cannot resist, but if we must go where temptation is within the path of duty, give us strength of spirit to meet it without fear.

For thine is the kingdom and the power and the glory forever and ever. Amen.

Lord, so in our hearts may we carry the knowledge that thy greatness is above us and that thy grace, through Jesus Christ, our Master, is sufficient for all our needs. Amen.

Since the Lord's Prayer can be broken down, it is our understanding that we know the basic rule for praying—knowing what to ask for—and here are four steps that are required when praying:

The first step is:

The prayer must be in Jesus' name. His name stands for Himself, for what he has done, his character, his blood given on Calvary, his power over death in the resurrection.

The second step is:

The prayer must be performed by a person in full touch of heart and habit and life with Jesus. That is the partnership basis.

The third step is:

There must be time spent habitually with the instruction book, the Old Book, the schoolbook on prayer. It broadens the vision, disciplines the judgment, emboldens the faith, and trains mind and heart and tongue. It is the Holy Bible.

The fourth step is:

In some quiet corner, there must be an actual praying day or time. Only through praying comes skill in praying, the skill of simplicity, of sureness of touch and of bold confidence.

Where shall we pray? In a quiet and personal place following the bidding of Jesus. "But thou, when thou prayest, enter into thy inner chamber, and when thou hast shut thy door, pray to thy Father which is in secret." The instructions are simple: The room should be remote from distraction, the door shut against noise, and the prayer so free from revealing that it is "secret." Jesus, himself, intent on quietness and sincerity, sometimes prayed on a mountainside, far into the night, or "rising up a great while before day departed into a solitary place, and there prayed." (Matt. 6:6)

The last question is: When shall we pray? At anytime, of course. God is not bound by occasions and seasons, and prayer is spontaneous, like any friendship. Anyone can pray in the middle of the night, in a car, on the bus, and in an airplane—even on a train. But, to this day, there are many people who feel that prayer can only be done in church. There is no limit except that of a man's own reluctance, timidity, or lack of the working agreement. Of course, the prayer must all be under the gracious guidance of the Holy Spirit.

Prayer enables us to communicate with the mysterious immensity of the spiritual world. It is by prayer that man reaches God and that God enters into him. Prayers appear to be indispensable to our highest development. No one should look upon prayer as an act in which only the weak-minded, the beggar, or coward indulge. "It is a shameful thing to pray," wrote Nietzche. In fact, it is no more shameful to pray than to drink or to breathe. Man needs God as he needs water and oxygen. Joined to intuition to the moral sense, to the sense of the beautiful and the light of intelligence, the sense of the holy gives to the personality its full flowering. There is no doubt that life's fulfillment demands the integral development of each of our activities; physiological, intellectual, affective, and spiritual. Spirit is, at the same time, reason and sentiment. We must, therefore, love the beauty of science and also the beauty of God. "In the beginning God created the heaven and the earth." (Gen. 1:1)

Where does faith fit in? "Now faith is the substance of things hoped for, the evidence of things not seen." (Heb. 11:1) Charles Ryrie, a twentieth century Bible scholar from Dallas Theological Seminary, who has his own study Bible says that,

"Faith give reality and proof of things unseen, treating them as if they were already objects of sight, rather than of hope." This brings us back to how and what prayers should be for. When Jesus prayed the Motto Prayer in Matthew, he prayed with faith that whatever he asked of the Father, the Father would grant it. Again, dealing with faith we are dealing with confidence, belief, loyalty, and, definitely, belief in God.

The Bible says, "But without faith it is impossible to please him: for he that cometh to God must believe that he is, and that he is rewarded of them that diligently seek him." (Heb. 11:7). The just and true shall live by faith. They give God everything, they uplift Him in prayer and faith.

Faith also comes with fasting. Daniel 9:3 says, "And I set my face unto the Lord God, to seek by prayer and supplication with fasting and sackcloth and ashes." Here Daniel tells us fasting comes with prayer, but prayer comes with faith. One can expound on faith but, to clearly state it, faith is believing. That is all. Man makes more out of faith than it really is. Faith is believing. Faith is believing that Jesus Christ is really the son of the Living God. Faith is acknowledgment. Richard Niebuhr, a twentieth century Protestant theologian and Professor of Theology and Christian Ethics at Yale University says that Christian social ethics rest, finally, in faith in the sovereign God who acts, not only through the church, but in the events of political, economic, and social life. Yet in faithful knowledge of God's mercy and sovereignty, goodness, and power, one dares to be a servant. Everyone lives in the condition of faith, for faith, in its elementary form, is not an appendage to life, but the inevitable form existence takes, because we are, in the deepest sense, contingent and dependent creatures. This unity, in large part, consists of our being together in a universe upon whose intricate and subtle operations, at all levels, we depend on absolutely. Christians live in faith because there is no other way in which they could live by.

Author Clyde A. Holbrook, a twentieth century clergyman and Theologian Professor of Religion at Oberlin College, also stated that we, through faith, subdued kingdoms, wrought righteousness, obtained promises, stopped the mouths of lions, quenched the power of fire, escaped the sword's edge, from weakness were made strong, were made mighty in war, and turned to flight armies of aliens. These modern day accomplishments parallel accomplishments in the Bible. God shut the mouths of Daniel's lions, made Abraham the Father of many natives, made David defeat the giant Goliath, and let Samson be mighty after his blindness. All of these things happened by the faith these men had in God. "Therefore being justified by faith, we have peace with God through our Lord

Jesus Christ." (Rom. 5:1) To understand faith, a person must understand believing. Without believing there is no faith. This brings us back to Hebrews 11:1, "Now faith is the substance of things hoped for, the evidence of things not seen."

Fasting now needs to be explained. Jesus fasted, and, when we think of him fasting, it was in the wilderness. "… and when He had fasted forty days and forty nights, He was afterward hungered." When Jesus fasted, he gave up all his bodily functions in the right capacity. He did it for strength, not for show. When he fasted, he fasted alone in the wilderness so he could focus on his purpose for fasting, and that was for strength.

Shirley Ross, the author of *Fasting*, explains that when a person fasts, it doesn't begin until two to three days after they stop eating. Technically, that is the moment when all the calories in the system are absorbed. At this point the body switches over from an external energy system to an internal circuit. In a sense, the deprivation of the normal incoming energy acts as a stimulus. When all calories are absorbed, you begin to have a negative calorie balance, and there is a moment of distinct change in metabolism. The term *metabolism* refers to the sum of all the physical and chemical processes that either produce and maintain living substance or break down matter in order to liberate heat for energy. The latter, the breaking down, is known as catabolism, one of the processes through which the body fuels itself during the fast. Also, when fasting for a long period of time, the body goes into a kind of hibernation period. The heart slows down, the body gets cold very easily, bowel movements practically cease, and the blood pressure drops. While the internal system is in operation, the body still must feed itself to supply fuel for its muscular activity and for the central nervous system. To accomplish these tasks, it mobilizes energy from various internal sources. Fats are commonly stored in what is known as adipose tissues.

When people start a fast, they feel that their fast has begun immediately, but a fast doesn't start until two to three days after a person stops eating. Therefore, when a person fasts for a day, they just aren't eating for this specific day.

When Jesus fasted for forty days and forty nights, his system was down from his normal self. Jesus was fasting for strength from his father. Jesus was fasting for his journey that awaited him.

Satan knew Jesus was weak in the flesh, but stronger in the spirit. Satan approached Jesus and said, "If thou be the Son of God, command that these stones be made bread." Jesus answered, "It is written, man shall not live by bread alone, but by every word that proceedeth out of the mouth of God." (Matt. 4:6)

The devil tried many times to tempt Christ in his weakness by taking him up to a holy city and setting him on a pinnacle of a temple, wanting Christ to prove that he was the Son of God. Then the devil took Christ up into an exceedingly high mountain and showed him all the kingdoms of the world and the glory of them, but in order for Christ to receive this package he had to fall down and worship Satan. "Jesus said unto Satan, it is written again, 'Thou shalt not tempt the Lord thy God.' Then saith Jesus unto Satan, 'Get thee hence, Satan. For it is written, thou shalt worship the Lord thy God, and Him only shalt thou serve.'" (Matt. 4:7-10)

As Jesus was fasting all this time, it was surely for strength because Satan tempted him three times. Even though those temptations might have looked good, it was his strength through God which defeated Satan. That is why he said "Get thee hence, Satan," or get behind me. There is nothing you can give me that my heavenly father cannot do for me. The devil knew he had lost. "Then the devil leaveth Him, and behold, angels came and ministered unto Him." (Matt. 4:1-11)

Even though this chapter's nature seems very easy to read and understand; lots of things don't come easily. During my studies and time working with a great variety of people, I have learned that people don't know how to pray. When they have prayed they don't have the faith to believe in what they are praying for. Authors can write everything down in black and white, but, if what the reader is trying to comprehend doesn't come out in color, something is wrong. One must go back and check themselves to see what went wrong. The saddest incident can happen when people put pride over knowledge. Instead of studying, people today would rather hear things by word of mouth, without finding the truth for themselves. One must not forget that fasting relies on strength to get us through our obstacles. Remember: Prayer, Fasting and Faith— What These Wonders Can Really Accomplish!

WHY IS THE WORD OF GOD A MOCKERY TO THE DYSFUNCTIONAL SOCIETY?

Why is the Word of God a mockery to the dysfunctional society? Society as a whole doesn't believe God at his word. Anytime society wants to take God's Word and try to manifest his own lifestyle and means, it is dysfunctional. Regardless of what religion and wrongful activities they encounter in this dysfunctional society, they believe that, at the end of their journey, everyone will go to heaven.

Jesus said in John 3:16-18, "For God so loved the world that He gave His only begotten Son, that whosoever believeth in Him should not perish, but have everlasting life." Jesus also said, "For God sent not His Son into the world to condemn the world; but that the world through Him might be saved. He that believeth on Him is not condemned, but he that believeth not is condemned already, because he hath not believed in the name of the only begotten Son of God." Jesus tells us in his words that if any man doesn't accept him as being the Son of the Living God, then they don't accept God the Father, which is in Heaven. (John 14:6)

Society fails to realize that only Jesus can save man and offer eternal life in heaven with his heavenly Father. John 14:6 says, "Jesus sayeth unto him, 'I am The Way, The Truth and The Life. No man cometh unto the Father, but by Me.'"

Society is dysfunctional today because of the different religions that try to rule the world with good and kind words. Cults are examples of misrepresentations of the Word of God to the dysfunctional society. Jesus Christ is the gospel and a cult is "any religious organization that says God called them to preach his word and that neglects the gospel of Jesus Christ."

THE JEHOVAH'S WITNESS
THEORY OF THE WORD OF GOD

The Jehovah's Witnesses are one of the largest denominations today that teach an untruthful doctrine according to the Bible. They believe that God's personal name is Jehovah. (*The Truth Shall Make You Free*, p. 17) The Bible lets us know God has many other names other than Jehovah.

Elohim . . . . "Strong One" (Genesis 1:1)

El Elyon . . . . "Most High" (Genesis 14:22)

El Olam . . . . "Everlasting God" (Genesis 21:33)

El Shaddai . . . . "Almighty God" (Genesis 17:1)

Adonai . . . . "Master" (Joshua 5:14)

Yahweh . . . . "I am the One who is" (Exodus 3:14)

Kurios . . . . "Lord" (Matthew 5:33)

Despoter . . . . "Master" (Acts 4:24)

Pater . . . . "Father" (John 4:24)

Elohim is the Hebrew word which is the plural of majesty, and it doesn't mean that He is mysteriously a trinity. (*Heavens and New Earth*, p. 36) The Jehovah's Witnesses define the Trinity as The God-head of orthodox Christian belief constructed by the person of the Father, the Son, and the Holy Spirit. The Bible addresses this truth in Genesis 1:26 "And God said, let us make man in our own image ..." *Us* meaning Father, the Son, and the Holy Spirit. Us is plural, not singular. The Father is called God. (1 Cor. 8:6) As individual roles, each can be called God; and collectively they can be spoken of as one God, because of their perfect unity. "But to us there is but one God, the Father, of whom are all things, and we in Him; and one Lord, Jesus Christ, by whom are all things, and we by Him" (1 Cor. 8:6) I'm distinctly describing the different attributes of God and the authority of the trinity through scripture. The Jehovah's Witnesses don't believe in the trinity, only God being just one, by himself.

Hebrews 1:8 discusses the Son in the trinity, "But unto the Son he saith, 'thy throne is forever; scepter of righteousness is the scepter of Thy kingdom.'" (John 20:28) "And Thomas answered and said unto him, 'My Lord and my God. The Holy Spirit is called God.'" (Acts 5:3-4) "But Peter said, 'Ananias, why hath Satan filled thine heart to lie to the Holy Ghost, and to keep back part of the price of the land? While it remained, was it not in thine own? And after it was sold, was it not in thine own power? Why hast thou conceived this thing in thine heart? Thou has not lied unto men, but unto God.'"

Again, we see the power of God identifying

himself as the Holy Spirit, the third person of the Godhead. Jesus is the "only begotten son" that God brought forth, because there are no other sons. The Jehovah Witnesses' believe that when they say "sons", they mean equal to Christ Jesus, being born and doing everything Jesus did, being without sin.

Charles Russel, the founder of the Jehovah's Witnesses, felt that he had the same power as Jesus, and so he started his own religion for this reason.

In 1914 Charles Russel told his followers to meet him on a mountain top to await the return of Christ. People sold their property and all that they had. Charles told them that Jesus would return at midnight. The people were waiting, and, after midnight, the people said we are still here. Well what happened to Christ? The Bible says, "But of that day and hour knoweth no man, no, not the angels of heaven, but my Father only." (Matt. 24:36). Charles Russel played it off by saying that Jesus did come, that he came and took their souls. He told them that they really went to heaven. However, when Charles Russel died, he failed to rise on the third day, as Jesus did. He convinced his believers that he did. He promised his followers they would no long suffer and that after he died he would be back to receive them. Now that doesn't make any sense. His theory does not correlate with the Word of God. Christians who follow the Bible have an idea of when Christ is going to return.

Matthew 24:29-31 says, "Immediately after the tribulation of those days shall the sun be darkened, and the moon shall not give her light, and the stars shall fall from heaven and the powers of the heavens shall be shaken. And then shall appear the sign of the Son of man in Heaven: and then shall all the tribes of the earth mourn, and they shall see the Son of man coming in the clouds of heaven with power and great glory. And He shall send his angels with a great sound of a trumpet, and they shall gather together his elect from the four winds from one end of heaven to the other." Revelation 1:7 further states, "Behold, he cometh with clouds; and every eye shall see Him, and they also which proceed Him: And all kindreds of the earth shall wail because of Him. Even so, Amen."

It is very clear no one knows when Christ is coming, so we cannot determine his exact return. Charles Russel thought that because he was one of the Sons of God he could determine the return of Christ. Again this backs up my statement that it takes man's theory and God's Word for man to come up with his own interpretation, and this is the most dangerous theory man can ever come up with. He was wrong in giving false information to feeble-minded individuals gullible to accept any information without searching for the right answers themselves. "For I testify unto every man that heareth the words of the prophecy of this book, If any man shall add unto these things, God shall add unto him the plagues that are written in this book. And if any man shall take away from the Words of the book of this prophecy, God shall take away his part out of the book of life, and out of the holy city, and from the things which are written in this book," states Revelation 22:18-19. So, as we decipher the differences of God's Word against the Jehovah's Witnesses theory, Christian Science, Spiritualism, Armstrongism, Mormonism, Eastern Mysticism, The Way International, Unity and the Unification Church, we can know that God's Word is much stronger than their doctrines.

GOD

God's personal name is Jehovah *(The Truth Shall Make You Free*, p. 17).

Only Jehovah is from everlasting to everlasting *(Make Sure of All Things*, [1965], p. 486).

Jesus Christ is not One God with the Father *(MS*, p. 485).

Holy Spirit is God's Active Force, not a person *(MS*, p. 487).

There was a time when Jehovah was alone in universal space. All life and energy and thought were contained in him alone *(Let God Be True* [1952], p. 25).

The obvious conclusion is that Satan is the originator of the trinity doctrine *(LG,* p. 101).

The Hebrew word *Elohim* is the plural of majesty. It does not mean that he is mysteriously a trinity *(New Heavens and New Earth,* p. 36).

JESUS CHRIST

Jesus Christ is not Jehovah God. He was the first son that Jehovah God brought forth *(LG,* p. 32).

The First Creation by God *(MS,* p. 282).

Jesus Christ had a pre-human existence *(LG,* p. 34).

Michael the archangel is no other than the only-begotten Son of God, now Jesus Christ *(NH,* p. 30).

Jesus was born about Oct. 1, B.C. 2, of the virgin Mary *(LG,* p. 36).

At baptism Jesus was anointed to become the Messiah, of Jesus the Christ (Anointed) *(LG,* p. 38).

He showed his subjection to God by humbling himself to a most disgraceful death on a torture stake *(LG,* p. 35).

God raised him as a mighty immortal spirit Son *(LG,* p. 40).

Christ was not raised in flesh, but with a spiritual body *(MS,* p. 426).

HOLY SPIRIT

The holy spirit is the invisible active force of

Almighty God which moves his servants to do his will *(LG,* p. 108).

SIN

Sin is a falling short of God's mark of perfection, transgression of His righteous law *(MS,* p. 456).

Adam and Eve sinned by disobeying God's plainly stated law *(MS,* p. 457).

At death, Adam was to return to the dust, a return to non-existence *(NH,* p. 88).

No descendant of Adam is free from sin: all inherit it from first man *(MS,* p. 458).

All are born in sin (imperfect, with wayward tendencies) *(MS,* p. 456).

Adam brought death not only upon himself, but also upon all the race descended from him *(NH,* p. 89).

REDEMPTION AND SALVATION

Adam is not included in those ransomed. He had perfect life, and this he deliberately forfeited *(LG,* p. 119).

Jesus Christ laid down in sacrifice a perfect HUMAN LIFE, equal to that which Adam forfeited *(You May Survive Armageddon,* p. 39).

The ransom, or redemptive price with which redemption is made, is "the man Christ Jesus" *(LG,* p. 113).

His perfect human life with all its rights and prospects, was laid down in death, but NOT FOR SIN AND IN PUNISHMENT *(LG,* p. 116). (Jesus was raised a divine spirit creature).

That which is redeemed or bought back is perfect human life with its rights and earthly prospects *(LG,* p. 114).

The value of the perfect human life was now available for use on behalf of faithful men *(LG,* p. 116).

Thus, makes possible general resurrection for mankind with opportunity for eternal life *(MS,* p. 4110).

The Bible plainly shows that 144,000 will share in heavenly glory, while the others will enjoy the blessings of life down here on earth *(LG,* p. 298).

All who by reason of faith in Jehovah God and in Christ Jesus dedicate themselves to do God's will and then faithfully carry out their dedication will be rewarded with everlasting life *(LG,* p. 298).

An unnumbered crowd of faithful persons do not expect to go to heaven. They have been promised everlasting life on earth if they prove their faithfulness *(LG,* p. 231), by faith in Jehovah's baptism, "provided … they abide in him, keeping their good conscience through faith and loyal service" *(NH,* p. 311).

Armageddon survivors and the mass of humankind will find life here on earth amid paradise conditions *(LG,* p. 279).

It is a gross twisting of the Scriptures to throw Jesus' words of John 3:3 to make them embrace all mankind *(The Watchtower,* Nov. 15, 1954, p. 68). This "great crowd" of people are not "born again," nor do they need to be "born again," because they gain everlasting life on the earth (Ibid., p. 682).

RETRIBUTION

The doctrine of a burning hell where the wicked are tortured eternally after death cannot be true *(LG,* p. 99).

A dead person is unconscious, inactive. The soul (entire being) itself is DEAD *(MS,* p. 143).

The millennial judgment day (the 1,000-year judgment day) will take place after Armageddon *(LG,* p. 284-286).

The final test will come by the loosing of Satan out of his restraint (at the end of the Millennium) *(LG,* p. 293).

Those supporting Satan (at the end of Millennium) will, with the Devil himself, be cast into the "lake of fire and sulphur." They are drowned in everlasting destruction (annihilated) and for them there is no resurrection *(LG,* p. 270).

All who reject the Kingdom message will be destroyed (LG, p. 190; YM, p. 341).

CHRISTIAN SCIENCE

In order to understand the Christian Science Foundation we must understand its foundation. Dr. Richard Cabot of the Massachusetts General Hospital stated that the reason for the group's success is, "That many patients have been driven into Christian Science by a multitude of shifting and mistake diagnosis, by the gross abuse of drugs, especially of morphine, and by the total neglect of rational psychotherapy on the part of many physicians ... the success of the Christian Science movement is due largely to the ignorance and narrow-mindedness of a certain proportion of the medical profession."

The Christian Scientists believe that The Virgin Mother conceived the idea of God and gave to her ideal the name of Jesus. Jesus was the offspring of Mary's self-conscious communion with God. (*SH*, 29:17-18, 32; 30:1) That the human Jesus was, or is, eternally not one with the Father ... but fleshly ... Christ is "the ideal Truth," "Divine Idea," "Reflection of God." This idea is not a true fact. The Bible says: "But while he thought on these things, behold, the angel of the Lord appeared unto him in a dream, saying, 'Joseph, thou son of David, fear not to take unto thee Mary thy wife: for that which is conceived in her is of the Holy Ghost. And she shall bring forth a son, and thou shalt call his name Jesus: for he shall save his people from their sins. Behold, a virgin shall be with child, and shall bring forth a son, and they shall call his name Emmanuel, which being interpreted is, God with us.'" (Matt. 1:20, 21, 23)

Christian Scientists believe that Jesus is the human man and Christ is the divine ideal. (*SH*, 473:15-16) This denomination also believe that the dual personality, Man-Christ, Jesus, continued to exist in the eternal order of Divine Science taking away the sins of the world. They also say that the disciples believed Jesus to be dead while he was in the sepulcher, whereas he was alive. (*SH*, 44:28-29) They feel that if Jesus never existed, it would have never made a difference. Christians know that Christ made a big difference in this world. Without him, the world wouldn't be saved and John 3:16-17 tells us this. It is Jesus Christ who brings humans back into communication with God, the Father.

In Matthew, Chapters 27 and 28 refute the notion that Christ Jesus is a dual personality. Christian Scientists also believe that the Holy Spirit is a divine science. They support this theory with: "the Spirit of God moved upon the face of the waters." The Divine Science, the Word of God, "sayeth to the darkness upon the face of error, 'God is All-in-All.'"

Christian Scientists feel God is infinite; the only life, substance, spirit, or soul; the only intelligence of the universe, including man. (*SH*, 330:11) Mary Baker Eddy, herself, said that God is "the ever-present, I am, filling all space, including in itself all mind, the one Father-Mother God." (*Rudimentary Divine Science*, p. 3:26, 4:1)

There are other issues that differ with the Bible, such as: Hell is "mortal belief, error, remorse, hatred, revenge, sin, sickness, death, that which worketh abomination or maketh a lie." (*SH* 588:1-4) The Bible says, "And death and hell were cast into the lake of fire. This is the second death. And whomever was not found written in the book of life was cast into the lake of fire." (Rev. 20:11) Hell is real, not a made up, fictional place. "Death is an illusion, the lie of life in matter; the unreal and untrue." (*SH* 584:9-10) "Wherefore, as by one man sin entered into the world, and death by sin; and so death passed upon all men, for that all have sinned." (Rom. 5:12) Death is not an illusion—it is factual, it is real! "And as it is appointed unto men once to die, but after this the judgment." (Heb. 9:22) "But why dost thou judge thy brother? Or why dost thou set at naught thy brother? For we shall all stand before the judgment sent of Christ. For it is written, as I live; saith the Lord, every knee shall bow to me, and every tongue shall confess to God. So then every one of us shall give account of himself to God." (Rom. 14:10-12).

The body cannot die, because matter has no life to surrender. (*SH* 426:30-31) Christian Scientists also believe that no final judgment awaits mortals, for the judgment day of wisdom comes hourly and continually. (*SH* 291:18-19) They express that if man shouldn't progress after death but should remain in error, he would be inevitably self-annihilated. (Misc. writing, p. 2) Also the only way to escape the misery of sin is to cease sinning. (*SH* 327:12-13) Let's not ignore their theory of Jesus dying; the material blood of Jesus was no more efficacious to cleanse from sin when it was shed upon the accused tree than when flowing in his veins as he went daily about His Father's business. (*SH* 25:6-9)

The difference between Christian Science and other religions is that the former claims that God exists due to matter. Christians, however, know that matter has no thoughts, feelings, emotions, actions, and ideas; therefore, how can God be filling up time and space due to matter? If God has no theory how could he know he's filling up space and time? They try to justify that God is matter, but God is filled with Spirit and truth.

GOD

God is All-In-All *(Science and Health,* 113:16). God, Spirit, being all, nothing is matter

(SH, 113:18).

God is incorporeal, divine, supreme, infinite Mind, Spirit, Soul, Principle, Life, Truth, Love *(SH,* 465:9).

God is infinite, the only Life, substance, Spirit, or Soul. The only intelligence of the universe, including man *(SH,* 330:11).

Life, Truth, and Love constitute the triune Person called God—God the Father-Mother; Christ the spiritual idea of sonship; Divine Science or the Holy Comforter *(SH,* 331:26-31).

God is "the ever-present, I am, filling all space, including in itself all Mind, the one Father-Mother God" (M.B. Eddy, *Rudimentary Divine Science,* pp. 3:26; 4:1).

The theory of three persons in one God (that is, a personal Trinity or Tri-unity) suggests polytheism, rather then the one everpresent I am *(SH,* 256:9-11).

JESUS CHRIST

Jesus is the human man and Christ is the divine idea *(SH,* 473:15-16).

If there had never existed such a person as the Galilean Prophet, it would make no difference to me *(First Church of Christ Scientist & Misc.,* pp. 318-19).

The virgin mother conceived this idea of God and gave to her ideal the name of Jesus. Jesus was the offspring of Mary's self-conscious communion with God *(SH,* 29:17-18, 32; 30:1).

Not that the human Jesus was or is eternal … not one with the father … but fleshly … Christ is "the ideal Truth," "Divine Idea," "reflection of God."

The dual personality (Christ Jesus) continued until the ascension, when Jesus disappeared, while Christ continues to exist in the eternal order of Divine Science taking away the sins of the world *(SH,* 333:32; 334:1).

His disciples believed Jesus to be dead, while he was in the sepulchre, whereas he was alive *(SH,* 44:28-29).

To the apprehension (of his students) our Master rose from the grave on the third day of his ascending though *(SH,* 509:4-7).

Resurrection is spiritualization of thought *(SH,* 593:9).

HOLY SPIRIT

Holy Ghost is Divine Science; the development of eternal Life, Truth, and Love *(SH,* 588:78).

In the words of St. John: "He shall give you another Comforter …" This Comforter I understand to be Divine Science *(SH,* 55:27-29).

The Spirit of God moved upon the face of the waters, (that is) Divine Science, the Work of God, saith to the darkness upon the face of error, "God is All In All" *(SH, 503:8-14)*.

SIN

Here also is found the cardinal point in Christian Science, that matter and evil (including all in harmony, sin, disease, and death) are UNREAL *(Misc. Writings,* p. 27).

Man is incapable of sin, sickness, and death *(SH, 475:28)*.

The real man cannot depart from holiness *(SH, 475:29)*.

Sin, sickness, and death are to be classified as effects of error. Christ came to destroy the belief of sin *(SH, 473:4-6)*.

Evil is unreal *(SH, 339:9-10)*.

The only reality of sin, sickness, or death is the awful fact that unrealities seem real to human, erring belief, until God strips off their disguise *(SH, 472:27-19)*.

The opposite of Truth, called error, sin, sickness, disease, death, is the false testimony of false material sense, of mind in matter *(SH, 108:24-26)*.

REDEMPTION

Jesus aided in reconciling man to God by giving man a truer sense of Love and this redeems man from the law of matter, sin, and death by the law of the Spirit *(SH, 19:6-10)*.

Jesus of Nazareth taught and demonstrated man's oneness with the Father *(SH, 18:3-4)*.

The efficacy of the crucifixion lay in the practical perfection and goodness it demonstrated for mankind *(SH, 24:27-28)*.

Atonement is the exemplification of man's unity with God *(SH, 18:1-2)*.

One sacrifice, however great, is insufficient to pay the debt of sin *(SH, 23:3-4)*.

The way to escape the misery of sin is to cease sinning. There is no other way *(SH, 327:12-13)*.

SALVATION

The material blood of Jesus was no more efficacious to cleanse from sin when it was shed upon the accursed tree than when flowing in his veins as he went daily about his Father's business *(SH, 25:6-9)*.

Salvation is Life, Truth, and Love understood and demonstrated as supreme over all; sin, sickness, and death destroyed *(SH, 593:20-22)*.

Sin, sickness, and death must be deemed as devoid of reality as they are of good, God *(SH, 525:28, 29)*.

To get rid of sin through Science, is to divert sin of any supposed mind or reality, and never to admit that sin can have intelligence or power, pain or pleasure. You conquer error by denying its verity *(SH,* 339:28-31).

Jesus taught the way of Life by demonstration. There is but one way to heaven; harmony and Christ in Divine Science shows us this way *(SH,* 242:9-10; 244-5).

RETRIBUTION

Hell is "Mortal belief, error, lust, remorse, hatred, revenge, sin, sickness, death ... that which worketh abomination or maketh a lie" *(SH,* 588:1-4).

No final judgment awaits mortals. For the judgment day of wisdom comes hourly and continually *(SH,* 291:28-29).

Sin makes its own hell, and goodness its own heaven *(SH,* 196:18-19).

Death is an illusion, the lie of life in matter; the unreal and untrue *(SH,* 584:9-10).

The body cannot die, because matter has no life to surrender *(SH,* 426:30-31).

Universal salvation rests on progression and probation *(SH,* 291:12).

If man should not progress after death, but should remain in error, he would be inevitably self-annihilated *(Misc. Writings,* p. 2).

THE UNITY CHURCH

The Unity Church began with the "healing" of Myrtle Fillmore. Its first fruits were the healing of her friends and neighbors, accomplished by realization of the Christ power within. (*SU*, p. 14) The Unity Church has a saying they use to reach people to come their denomination. The Unity Church feels that truth is taught in all religions, simplified and systematized so everyone can understand and apply it. (Freeman, *The Story of Unity*, p. 61)

According to the Unity Church, God isn't a person that has life, intelligence, love, or power. God instead is invisible, intangible, but very real and something called life. The Unity doesn't believe God to be a person. God is the total of all good, whether manifested or unexpressed. (Cady. *Lesson in Truth*, p. 6) Christians teach the true Word of God. Acts 17:11 says "These were more noble than those in Thessalonica, in that they received the word with all readiness of mind, and searched the scriptures daily, whether those things were so." This scripture returns us to II Timothy 2:15. "Study to show thyself approved unto God, a workman that needeth not to be ashamed, rightly dividing the Word of Truth." Charles Ryrie is a biblical scholar and twentieth century college professor from Dallas Theological Seminary who says when a person studies then they must—and rightly—"Be Diligent," dividing, or, correctly handling the Word of God, in both analysis and presentation: false teachers directly contrast the ideal way of studying. (p. 17.9 in his footnotes of his Study Bible)

Unity Church believes the Hottentot, or the truest heathen that ever lived, who worshiped the golden calf as his highest conception of God, worshiped God. (*LT*, p. 126, Cited in Martin p. 279)

The Word of God says in Exodus 20:3-5, "Thou shalt have no other gods before me. Thou shalt not make unto thee any graven image, or any likeness of anything that is in heaven above or that is in the earth beneath, or that is in the water under the earth: Thou shalt not bow down thyself to them, not serve them: For I, the Lord thy God am a jealous God visiting the iniquity of the fathers upon the children unto the third and fourth generation of them that hate me." God won't share his worship with anything or anyone and Exodus 20:23 says, "Ye shall not make with me gods of silver, neither shall ye make unto you gods of gold." God never replaced himself with a golden calf and any statement otherwise is false—false doctrine.

God isn't a person having life, intelligence, love, and power. Again, John 1:1, and John 1:14, John 3:16-

17 answer this question. But why does the Unity Church feel that God is matter? The reason is because they don't have the answer to how God was created. The Unity Church also feel that God is the substance, or real thing, standing under every visible form of life, love, intelligence, or power. Each rock, tree, animal—everything visible—is a manifestation of the numberless manifestations or individualities and each contains the whole. (*LT*, p. 8-9, cited in Martin, p. 281) Unitarians also say that God is the always present, indwelling mind—the Father within you ... is in the spiritual realms which underlie all creative forces. (Fillmore, *The Science of Being and Christians Healing*, p. 9) God is Principal, Law, Being, Mind, Spirit, All Good, Omnipresent, Omniscient, Omnipotent, Unchangeable, Creator, Father, Cause, and Source of All That Is. (*SB*, p. 15) God Is. Man Is. We are now in the presence of that eternal Is-ness—Osiris and Isis are now our Father-Mother as fully as they were of Old Egypt. (*SB*, p. 229)

The definition of substance is matter, material, being, object, item, person, animal, something, element. Now when Unity Church teachings state God is the substance, Unitarians feel he is the Matter and the Element that make things exist. Matter has no thought, theory, love, nor intellectual capabilities of doing anything but standing still. Humans know that air exists but has no thought, but would humans say that air has love, thought, and intellectual abilities? John 4:24 says, "God is a Spirit; and they that worship Him must worship Him in spirit and in truth." A Christian must keep in mind that in most of the different dysfunctional religions the leaders hold such high positions as psychologists, biologists, and medical doctors. People who are trained to scientifically understand ideas are the kinds of people who try to figure out God, and, since they can't find the right answer, they change the form of the question. It's very common for people to change theories and get a vast majority of people to follow them. It's interesting that when Christ walked on this earth, whenever someone approached Christ, they would ask him who he was and Jesus would say, "Who do they say that I am?" Jesus had all the answers to the questions when people asked, he had past and present question answered. Whenever Jesus answered questions, all his answers related to God. When anyone asked these different religious organizations a certain question, the members would say that God gave them the answer.

The Unity Church says that the Krishna of the Hindu is the same as the Christos of the Greeks and the Messiah of the Hebrews. (*SB*, p. 22) Jesus has two distinct regions: the fleshly, mortal part which was Jesus, the Son of Man, and the central, living, real part which was Spirit, the Son of God, the Christ, the Anointed. Each one of us, according to the Unity, has two regions of being—the fleshly mortal and, at the very center of our being, there is the Christ Child, the Son of God, the Anointed in us. (Fillmore, *The Unity Treasure Chest*, p. 49) Christ, or perfect man ideally existing eternally in divine minds, is the true spiritual, higher-self of every individual. (*Metaphysical Bible Dictionary*, p. 150). This ideal that the Krishna of the Hindu is the same as the *Christos* of the Greeks is an untrue statement. Christians follow Christ the Unity sect follow Krishna. God and Christ are the same. "And the Word was made flesh, and dwelt among us; (and we beheld His glory, the glory as of the only begotten of the Father) full of grace and truth." (John 1:14) As Christians, when we get to heaven we will be spiritually knowledgeable. We are not on the same level as Christ Jesus. God dwells in us which is the Holy Spirit. "And they were all filled with the Holy Ghost, and began to speak with other tongues, as the Spirit gave them utterance." (Acts 2:4) The same Christ that lives within individuals lived in Jesus. It's the part of himself which God has put within humans and lives there. The Christ within humans is the "Beloved Son," the same as it was in Jesus. (*UTC*, p. 51)

The Unitarian doctrine of the Holy Spirit definition is the very spirit of truths lying latent within humans, each and every one. (*Unity Magazine*, February 1918) The Father is Principle, the Son is the Principal revealed in the creative plan, and the Holy Spirit is the executive power of both the Father and Son that carries out the plan. (*MBD*, p. 629) Spirit is substance, that invisible, intangible but real something which has its own indestructible core and stands under, or at the center of, every visible thing in existence. (Cady, *God a Present Help*, pp. 53-54)

UNITY

Unity is the truth that is taught in all religions, simplified and systematized so that anyone can understand and apply it (Freeman, *The Story of Unity*, p. 61).

Unity began with the "healing" of Myrtle Fillmore. Its first fruits were the healing of her friends and neighbors, accomplished by realization of the Christ Power within *(SU,* p. 14).

GOD

God is not a person having life, intelligence, love, power. God is that invisible, intangible, but very real, something we call life. God is the total ... of all good, whether manifested or unexpressed (Cady, *Lessons in Truth*, p. 6).

I believe the Hottentot, or the truest heathen that ever lived, he who worships the golden calf as his highest conception of God, worships God (*LT*, p. 126, cited in Martin, p. 279).

God is the always present, indwelling Mind. The Father within you ... is in the spiritual realms which underlie all creative forces (Fillmore, *The Science of Being and Christian Healing*, p. 9).

God is. Man is. We are now in the presence of that eternal Is-ness—Osiris and Isis are now our Father-Mother as fully as they were of old Egypt (*SB*, p. 229).

God is Principle, Law, Being, mind, Spirit, All Good, Omnipresent, Omniscient, Omnipotent, Unchangeable, Creator, Father, Cause and Source of all that is (*SB*, p. 15).

God is the substance, or real thing standing under every visible form of life, love, intelligence, or power. Each rock, tree, animal, everything visible is a manifestation of the numberless manifestations, or individualities. Each ... contains the whole (*LT*, pp. 8-9, cited in Martin, p. 281).

JESUS CHRIST

The Krishna of the Hindu is the same as the Christos of the Greeks and the Messiah of the Hebrews (*SB*, p. 22).

There were in the person of Jesus two distinct regions—the fleshly, mortal part which was Jesus, the son of man; then there was the central, living, real part which was Spirit, the Son of God, the Christ, the Anointed. So ... each one of us has two regions of being—the fleshly, mortal ... and at the very center of our being there is the ... Christ Child, the Son of God, the Anointed in us (Fillmore, *The Unity Treasure Chest,* p. 49).

This Christ or perfect-man idea existing eternally in divine mind is the true spiritual, higher-self of every individual *(Metaphysical Bible Dictionary,* p. 150).

This same Christ lives within us that lived in Jesus. It is the part of Himself which God has put within us, which ever lives there ... Christ, within us is the "beloved Son," the same as it was in Jesus *(UTC,* p. 51).

HOLY SPIRIT

Definition: The very spirit of truth lying latent within us, each and every one *(Unity Magazine,* February 1918).

The Father is Principle, the Son is that Principle revealed in the creative plan, the Holy Spirit is the executive power of both the Father and Son, carry out the plan *(MBD,* p. 629).

Spirit is substance ... that invisible, intangible but real something which as its indestructible core and cause stands under, or at the center of, every visible thing in existence (Cady, *God a Present Help*, pp. 53-54).

MAN AND SIN

Man is made in the image of God ... the divine spark at the center of his being ... is very part of God Himself *(GP*, p. 57).

God is within you. You can find Him there *(UTC*, p. 29).

Every man in reality, is the Son of God, not a Son of God. We are all one in the One Mind, and do not exist as individualities in Divine Mind. Man is the manifestation of the "only begotten Son" of God, or the Christ idea Man. Therefore he is the Christ of God *(UM*, February 1918, p. 127).

God is good and God is all. Therefore I refuse to believe in the reality of devil or evil in any of its forms ... God is life ... I refuse to believe in the reality of loss of life, or death ... I refuse to believe in inefficiency and weakness ... in ignorance, the reality of lack or poverty ... hate or revenge *(SB*, pp. 58-59).

In its virgin purity, [the flesh] is the immaculate substance of Being. If it appears corrupt, or subject to corruption, humanity has made it so through ignorance *(SB*, p. 208).

The forgiveness of sin is an erasure of mortal

thoughts from consciousness *(SB,* p. 56).

Sin, sickness, poverty, old age, and death are not real, and they have no power over me. There is nothing for me to fear *(LT,* p. 35).

REDEMPTION AND SALVATION

Jesus of Nazareth played an important part in opening the way for every one of us into the Father's kingdom. However, that was not through His death on the cross, but through His overcoming death (UTC, p. 67).

That which died upon the cross was the consciousness of all mortal believers that hold us in bondage—such as sin, evil, sickness, fleshly lusts, and death—which He overcame *(UTC,* pp. 68-69).

The error lies in the belief that He was the only begotten Son of God, and that He overcame for us, and that by simply believing on Him we are saved *(UTC,* pp. 68-69).

Paul is responsible for ... this throwing of the whole burden upon the blood of Jesus—that He was the great once-for-all bloody sacrifice, and that no other would ever be necessary. Jesus said ... "Follow me." He meant: do as I do. I have overcome, now by following in my footsteps you shall overcome *(UTC,* p. 69).

Being born again or from above is ... the establishment of that which had always existed as the perfect man idea of Divine Mind *(SB,* p. 25).

To "know thyself" is to know that you are I AM and not flesh and blood. It is this I AM that is born of the flesh and born of Spirit *(SB,* p. 206).

The eternal life taught and demonstrated by Jesus is not gained by dying, but by purifying the body until it becomes the undying habitation of the soul *(UM,* July 1922).

We believe the repeated incarnations of man to be a merciful provision of our loving Father to the end that all may have opportunity to obtain immortality through regeneration as did Jesus *(Unity Statement of Faith,* art. 22).

UNIFICATION CHURCH

The Unification Church is another denomination that does not follow the true Word of God. They believe humans have the means to heal all modern-day human souls and bring the Kingdom of God within the reach of every man. (*Man, Christianity in Crisis*, p. ix)

Unification believes God, himself said that the most basic and central truth of this universe is that God is the Father and humans are his children (*CIC*, p. 9) There is one living, eternal, and true God, a Person, beyond space and time ... source of all truth, beauty and goodness ... creator and sustainer of man and the universe. (*Declaration of Unification Theological Affirmations at Barrytown*, New York, October 14, 1976)

God, being the First Cause of all creation, also exists because of a reciprocal relationship between the dual characteristics of positivity and negativity ... the positivity and negativity of God are called "Masculinity" and "Femininity" respectively. (Moon, *Divine Principle*, p. 24) God existed as the internal masculine subject, and he created the universe as his external feminine object. (*DP*, p. 25) Man is the visible; and God is the invisible form. God and Man are one. Man is incarnate God ... as important in value as God himself. (*CIC*, p. 5) God is just like humans, and all human traits originate in God. (*CIC*, p. 4)

If everyone has the power to heal all modern-day human souls, and the Kingdom of God is reachable, then why is the world so chaotic? The Unification Church explains this by stating humans don't have the authority to heal human souls; only Christ can do this, and the Kingdom of God will come at hand when Christ returns for his children. If humans have all the power that the Unitarians claim, then humans wouldn't need God. This is just like Satan telling Eve that if she ate from the Tree of Knowledge of Good and Evil, she would be just as wise as God. What happened to Eve? She was banished from the Garden of Eden, and she didn't become wise; she became foolish.

God doesn't possess negativity. He hates sin. So dual positive and negative characteristics repudiate the Unitarian theory, and they say God has feminine characteristics only because God created male and female. God made female because male was lonely, and he requested it. Man was formed in the image of God, but woman was made from the rib of man. Femininity does not originate from God himself. He formed woman from man.

The Unification Church also believes that, as a man, Jesus was no different from the rest of mankind except for the fact that he was without original sin. (*DP*, p. 212) He was the one who lived God's ideal in fullest realization. (*CIC*, p. 12) He attained the purpose of creation. (*DP*, p. 290). In light of his attained deity, he could have been called God, and he can be called God. *(DP*, pp. 210-211) Jesus' death was neither his will nor his fault. It was murder and his body was taken by Satan. (*CIC*, p. 104). If he will come again as the third Adam, the Lord of the Second Advent, the Kingdom of God will gradually appear. (*DP*, p. 506)

Jesus arrived on the earth as the sinless, or perfect, Adam. His first mission was to restore his bride and form the first family of God, but he was crucified. Jesus Christ must come again to consummate the mission he didn't finish 2,000 years ago. (*CIC*, p. 27) Christ will be born in a country in the East and will place a seal on the foreheads of the 144,000 (*DP*, p. 520) Korea should be the nation that can receive the Lord of the second Advent. (*DP*, p. 520) And even in the spirit world, after his resurrection, he will live as a spirit man with his disciples. (*DP*, p. 212)

The Word of God definitely differs from the Unification Church teachings. "Now the birth of Jesus Christ was on this wise: When as His mother Mary was espoused to Joseph, before they came together, she was found with child of the Holy Ghost." (Matt. 1:18) Therefore the Lord Himself shall give you a sign;

Behold, a virgin shall conceive, and bear a son, and shall call his name Immanuel." (Isa. 7:14)

"And without controversy, great is the mystery of godliness: God was manifest in the flesh, justified in the spirit, seen of angels, preached unto the Gentiles, believed on in the world, received up into glory." (1 Tim. 3:16) "And the Word was made flesh, and dwelt among us, and we beheld His glory, the glory as of the only begotten of the Father, full of Grace and Truth." (John 1:14) "No man hath seen God at anytime, the only begotten Son, which is in the bosom of the Father, he hath declared Him." (John 1:18) "And declared to be the Son of God with power, according to the spirit of holiness, by the resurrection from the dead." (Rom. 1:4) "And if Christ be not raised, your faith is vain; ye are yet in your sins." (1 Cori. 15:17) "Wherefore he is able also to save them to the uttermost that come unto God by him, seeing he ever liveth to make intercession for them." (Heb. 7:25)

The Unification Church teachings say that Christ will come again as the Third Adam, however, 1 Corinthians 15:45-47 says, "And so it is written, the first man Adam was made a living soul; the last Adam was made a quickening spirit. Howbeit that was not first which is spiritual, but that which is natural; and afterward that which is spiritual. The first man is of the earth, earthly. The second man is the Lord from heaven."

The Third Adam needs to be explained from a scriptural view. "And so it is written, the first man Adam was made a living soul; the last Adam as made a quickening spirit." (1 Cor. 15:45) Man was made from the breath of God, and, Jesus, being God, manifested himself as the Third Adam. "And I stood upon the sand of the sea, and saw a beast rise up out of the sea, having seven heads and ten horns, and upon his horns ten crowns, and upon his heads the name of blasphemy." (Rev. 13:1) (The 'I' meaning the Apostle John—Charles Ryrie footnotes, p. 1772 and 1802 of his Study Bible.) Charles Ryrie, scholar in Bible translation and professor at Dallas Theological Seminary, translates the words of the Apostle John's as concerning the many emperors of Rome who defied themselves. But, the explanation continues, Antichrist will far outshine all his predecessors in his blasphemous ways. Ten horns—the ten kings that will give their power and authority to the Antichrist—and he will have demonic forces behind anti-Christian teachings and activities. People denied the reality of Christ's incarnation and his relationship to the Father. Satan will give the Antichrist his power. (Charles Ryrie footnotes). Revelation 13:2 says, "And the beast which I saw was like unto a leopard, and his feet were as the feet of a bear, and his mouth as the mouth of a lion: and the dragon gave him his power, and his seat, and great authority." Verse 3:

"And I saw one of his heads as it were wounded to death; and his deadly wound was healed: and all the world wondered after the beast." Verse 4: "And they worshiped the dragon which gave power unto the beast: and they worshiped the beast, saying 'Who is like unto the beast? Who is able to make war with him?'" Verse 5: "And there was given unto him a mouth speaking great things and blasphemies; and power was given unto him to continue forty and two months." Verse 6: "And he opened his mouth in blasphemy against God, to blaspheme His name, and his tabernacles and them that dwell in heaven." Verse 7: "And it was given unto him to make war with the saints, and to overcome them: and power was given him over all kindreds, and tongues, and nations." Verse 8: "And all that dwell upon the earth shall worship him, whose names are not written in the book of life of the Lamb slain from the foundation of the world." Verse 9: "If any man have an ear, let him hear."

Verse 10: "He that leadeth into captivity shall go into captivity: he that killeth with the sword must be killed with the sword. Here is the patience and the faith of the saints." Verse 11: "And I behold another beast coming up out of the earth; and he had two horns like a lamb, and he spake as a dragon." Verse 12: "And he exerciseth all the power of the first beast before him, and causeth the earth and them which dwell therein to worship the first beast, whose deadly wound was healed." Verse 13: "And he doeth great wonders, so that he maketh fire come down from heaven on the earth in the sight of men." Verse 14: "And deceiveth them that dwell on the earth by the means of those miracles which he had power to do in the sight of the beast; saying to them that dwell on the earth, that they should make an image to the beast, which had the wound by a sword, and did live." Verse 15: "And he had power to give life unto the image of the beast, that the image of the beast, that the image of the beast should both speak and cause that as many as would not worship the image of the beast should be killed."

Verse 16: "And he causeth all, both small and great, rich and poor, free and bound, to receive a mark in their right hand, or in their foreheads." Verse 17: "And that no man might buy or sell, save he that had the mark, or the name of the beast or the number of his name."

Verse 18: "Here is wisdom. Let him that hath understanding count the number of the beast: for it is the number of a man; and his number is six hundred, threescore and six."

The Unification Church is talking about the Third Adam as not Jesus Christ, but Satan, the Antichrist. Satan will perform wonders and reveal signs to make people follow his ways, and he will also do good works and deeds. This Third Adam, which is Satan, will mark them on the right hand and on their foreheads so they can buy goods. Now in today's society, people aren't marked with 666 on our hands or any other parts of their body so they can buy everyday necessities. Emotionally and mentally, this Antichrist will fill some of society's needs, and many will fall right into Satan's trap. This is how man will fall. Satan will be happy because he is going to have some followers; because at this time, people will be looking and searching for the truth. Christians must step in and understand God's will by studying, praying, fasting, and putting on the whole armor of God, not when they feel it's the right time or when everything's going wrong in their lives. Studying is hard for some people, but it is a very serious part of a Christian's life. Studying will let a Christian know that these issues will come at hand.

Jesus came in the form of a man, and he came as a mediator for God's people in order for anyone to get to God the Father. People must go through Christ Jesus, and this was accomplished when Jesus died on the cross for the whole world. He died for the sins of the world; his blood cleanses and forgives those who accept him as their personal Savior. The kingdom of God will come to hand when Christ comes back for his children. When Jesus died on the cross, Matthew 27:50

states, "Jesus when he had cried again with a loud voice, yielded up the ghost." Jesus willingly gave up the Ghost, there is nowhere that says Satan took Christ's body.

When Jesus rose, he went to his disciples. One thing he told them was the Great Commission, which is in Matthew 28:18-20: "And Jesus came and spake unto them, saying, 'All power is given unto me in heaven and in earth. Go ye therefore, and teach all nations, baptizing them in the name of the Father, and of the Son, and of the Holy Ghost teaching them to observe all things whatsoever I have commanded you: and lo, I am with you always, even unto the end of the world. Amen.'" Jesus' mission was accomplished with the Heavenly Father by dying on the cross and rising on the third day. The death of Jesus was the will of his Father. Matthew 26:39 states, "And he went a little farther, and fell on his face, and prayed, saying, 'Oh, my Father, if it be possible, let his cup pass from me: nevertheless not as I will, but as thou wilt.'" The cup of which Jesus spoke was all the suffering involved in the sinless Son of God taking upon Himself the sin of mankind. It also includes necessary, though temporary, separation from God. He naturally shrank from this, though he willingly submitted to it. (Footnotes from Charles Ryrie Study Bible, p. 1389)

The Unification Church teaches that Korea

should be the nation that can receive the Lord of the Second Advent. (*DP*, p. 520) Anybody today can accept Christ as their personal Savior. The Bible says, "That if thou shalt confess with thy mouth the Lord Jesus, and shalt believe in thine heart that God hath raised Him from the dead, thou shalt be saved." (Rom. 10:19) Korea is not the only nation that can be saved. Anybody today can accept Christ as their personal savior. The Apostle Paul reveals this fact in Romans 1:16, "For I am not ashamed of the gospel of Christ: For it is the power of God unto salvation to everyone that believeth; to the Jew first, and also to the Greek." By Jesus dying for the whole world, the whole world can be saved, and no one has to wait for certain times.

The Unification Church's theory about the Holy Spirit states that "The Holy Spirit is a female Spirit. She also cleanses the sins of the people in order to restore them, thus indemnifying the sin committed by Eve ..." the Holy Spirit, being female (negativity) in working on earth (*DP*, p. 215) The Holy Spirit is the Third Person of the God-head; the Holy Spirit is "He." Jesus said in John 14:16-17, "And I will pray to the Father, and He shall give you another comforter, that 'He' may abide with you forever; Even the Spirit of truth; whom the world cannot receive, because it seeth 'Him' not, neither knoweth 'Him:' but ye know Him; for 'He' dwelleth with you, and shall be in you." The quotations which are the author's indicate that Jesus reveals that the Holy Spirit is male. When it came to man's salvation, God took care of this by sending his only begotten Son. Therefore, the Holy Spirit's purpose on this earth is that he represents beliefs of Jesus Christ. He helps us recall the things Christ teaches us in His Word; He will teach us the difference between right and wrong. Also, the Holy Spirit gives us spiritual gifts, and he also lets us know Truth and Error.

When religious groups believe in theories like these, it makes a Christian wonder "Why?" The only answer to this question is that there is no theory or parable in the Word of God that backs up any idea other than the Truth.

UNIFICATION CHURCH

We now have the means to heal all modern-day human problems, exalt every human soul, and bring the Kingdom of God within the reach of every man (Moon, *Christianity in Crisis*, p. ix).

GOD

God Himself told me that the most basic and central truth of this universe is that God is the Father and we are His children *(CIC, p. 9)*.

There is one living, eternal, and true God, a Person, beyond space and time ... source of all truth, beauty, and goodness ... creator and sustainer of man and the universe *(Declaration of Unification Theological Affirmations at Barrytown,* New York, October 14, 1976).

God, being the First Cause of all creation, also exists because of a reciprocal relationship between the dual characteristics of positivity and negativity ... We call the positivity and negativity of God "masculinity" and "femininity" respectively (Moon, *Divine Principle,* p. 24).

God existed as the internal masculine subject, and He created the universe and His external feminine object *(DP,* p. 25).

Man is the visible; and God is the invisible form. God and man are one. Man is incarnate God ... as important in value as God Himself *(CIC,* p. 5).

God is just like you and me. All human traits originate in God *(CIC,* p. 4).

JESUS CHRIST

As a man [Jesus was] no different from us except for the fact that he was without original sin *(DP,* p. 212).

He was the one who lived God's ideal in fullest realization *(CIC,* p. 12).

He "attained" the purpose of creation *(DP,* p. 290).

In light of his attained deity he may well be called God. Nevertheless, he can by no means be called God Himself *(DP,* pp. 210-11).

The death of Jesus was neither his will nor his fault. [It was] murder, and his body was taken by Satan *(CIC,* p. 104).

He will come again as the third Adam, the lord of the Second Advent. The Kingdom of God will gradually appear *(DP,* p. 506).

Jesus came as the sinless Adam, or perfected Adam. His first mission was to restore his bride and form the first family of God. But he was crucified. Jesus Christ must come again to consummate the mission he left undone 2,000 years ago *(CIC,* p. 27). See "Reincarnation."

Christ will be born in a country in the East … and will place a seal on the foreheads of the 144,000 *(DP*, p. 520).

Korea should be the nation that can receive the Lord of the Second Advent *(DP,* p. 520).

Even in the spirit world after his resurrection, he lives as a spirit man with his disciples *(DP,* p. 212).

HOLY SPIRIT

The Holy Spirit is a female Spirit. She also cleanses the sins of the people in order to restore them, thus indemnifying the sin committed by Eve … the

Holy Spirit, being female (negativity) in working on earth *(DP*, p. 215).

There must be a True Mother with the True Father, in order to give rebirth to fallen children as children of goodness. She is the Holy Spirit *(DP*, p. 215).

SIN

Adam and Eve ... were tempted by the archangel Lucifer into illicit and forbidden love. Through this, Adam and Eve willfully turned away from God's will and purpose for them, thus bringing themselves and the human race into spiritual death *(DUTA)*.

Evil is the emergence of selfishness into this world. God's principle of unselfish giving was twisted into an ungodly principle of selfish taking. The origin of evil is Satan *(CIC*, pp. 16-17).

REDEMPTION AND SALVATION

God's will that all people be restored to Him is predestined absolutely, and He has elected all people to salvation *(DUTA)*.

He [Jesus] must come again to consummate the mission he left undone 2,000 years ago. He was crucified ... not given a chance to restore his bride *(CIC*, p. 27).

God's work has been the restoration of original goodness ... To do this job God needs certain tools. The religions of the world have served as these tools for God ... Christianity may be considered the most advanced and progressive religion because it teaches this sacrificial love and duty in supreme form *(CIC, pp. 17-18)*.

Christ will come as before, as a man in the flesh, and he will establish a family through marriage to his Bride, a woman in the flesh and they will become the True Parents of all mankind. Through our accepting the True Parents (the Second Coming of Christ), obeying them and following them, our original sin will be eliminated and we will eventually become perfect *(DUTA)*.

Marriage is the most important means of establishing God's kingdom on earth *(CIC, p. 25)*.

God intended to make Adam and Eve one in heavenly matrimony. Then they would have borne sinless children and become the true mother and father for all mankind ... establishing the heavenly kingdom on earth *(CIC, p. 26)*.

RESURRECTION AND ETERNAL LIFE

The invisible world was not created after the fall ... it had been created before the creation of men, so that their spirits, after they had accomplished the purpose of creation, might go and live there forever, once they had discarded their flesh, after their physical life on earth *(DP,* p. 168).

Physical [death] is not a result of the fall ... spiritual death signifying the degradation to Satanic dominion, is the real death caused by the fall *(DP,* p. 169).

The human body, once it is dissolved into dust, cannot be resurrected to its original state. It is not necessary for a spirit man to resume his flesh, when there is a vast spirit world where he is supposed to go and live forever *(DP,* p. 170).

Therefore, "resurrection," means the phenomena occurring in the process of man's restoration ... When we repent of our sins, making ourselves better and better, day by day, we are coming closer to resurrection *(DP,* p. 170).

Paradise is the region of the spirit world where those spirit men who have attained the life-spirit stage by believing in Jesus while on earth go after death, and stay until the gate to the Kingdom of Heaven is opened *(DP,* p. 177).

The providence of restoration, beginning on the individual level, is headed for the final goal of the restoration of the entire cosmos *(DP,* p. 187).

REINCARNATION

The spirit men who left their missions unaccomplished on earth descend to earthly men ... and

cooperate with them for the accomplishment of the will
… In this case, the earthly man is the "second coming"
of the spirit man … John the Baptist … had to accomplish the mission Elijah had left unaccomplished *(DP,
pp.* 187-88).

MORMONS

Another interesting denomination in today's society is Mormonism. Mormons believe in God the Eternal Father, in his son Jesus Christ and in the Holy Ghost (*Articles of Faith*, p. 1), and this cannot be construed to mean that the Father, the Son and the Holy Ghost are one in substance and in person (Talmage, *Articles of Faith*, p. 40) Mormons teach there are three Gods ... separate in personality, united in purpose, in plan, and in all attributes of perfection. (McConkie, *Mormon Doctrine*, p. 270)

God is an organized being just as those are who are in the flesh. He is a progressive being and possesses the capacity of eternal increase, perhaps once a child and mortal like ourselves. (*Gospel Doctrine*, p. 64, *Articles of Faith*, p. 529; *Journal of Discourses*, 1:123) The Father has a body of flesh and bones as tangible as man's. (*Doctrine and Covenants*, 130:22) God is not omnipresent, cannot be "physically present in more than one place at a time." (Talmage, *DC*, p. 48) Every man who reigns in celestial glory is a god to his dominions. (McConkie, *MD*, p. 322) There never was a time when there were not Gods and worlds. (Young, *Discourses*, pp. 22-33) Each god, through his wife or wives, raises up a numerous family of sons and daughters. (Pratt, *The Seer*, 1, no. 3, p. 37) The doctrine of a plurality of Gods is prominent in the Bible. The heads of the Gods appointed our God for us. (*Teaching of the Prophet Joseph Smith*, pp. 370-72) The eternal Father is a progressive Being, the capacity of eternal increase. (Talmage, *DC*, p. 529) Mormons say that they believe in God, the Father, and in his son Jesus Christ, and in the Holy Spirit. The Mormons don't believe in the Trinity; they believe that the three parts of God are separate, not connected, and one.

The Mormon's beliefs are the same as the Jehovah's Witnesses'. Due to humans' open minds, the majority of society took prayer out of schools. Without prayer in an institution that needs strength and guidance, the children's hope for the school year goes down from 100% hopeful to 30% of a chance. Let's examine the school system today in New York City. They are trying to get the system to teach homosexuality in the classrooms instead of putting prayer back in school—a very good example of our society going downhill. Putting prayer back into our school systems will help anyone cope with the struggles in today's society, and, for Christians, eliminating the impossible is always possible; because the truth and power lies in Jesus Christ.

GOD

We believe in God the Eternal Father, and in His son Jesus Christ, and in the Holy Ghost *(Articles of Faith,* p. 1).

This cannot rationally be construed to mean that the Father, the Son and the Holy Ghost are one in substance and in person (Talmage, *Articles of Faith,* p. 40).

There are three Gods ... separate in personality, united in purpose, in plan, and in all attributes of perfection (McConkie, *Mormon Doctrine,* p. 270).

God is an organized being just as we are who are now in the flesh. He is a progressive being, and possesses the capacity of eternal increase. Perhaps once a child and mortal like ourselves *(Gospel Doctrine,* p. 64; AF, p. 529; *Journal of Discourses,* 1:123).

The Father has a body of flesh and bones as tangible as man's *(Doctrine and Covenants,* 130:ZZ).

God is not omnipresent ... cannot be "physically present in more than one place at a time" (Talmage, *DC,* p. 48).

Every man who reigns in celestial glory is a god to his dominions (McConkie, *MD,* p. 322).

There never was a time when there were not Gods and worlds (Young, *Discourses,* pp. 22-23).

Each god, through his wife or wives, raises up a

numerous family of sons and daughters (Pratt, *The Seer*, 1, no. 3, p. 37).

The doctrine of a plurality of Gods is prominent in the Bible. The heads of the Gods appointed our God for us *(Teaching of the Prophet Jos. Smith*, pp. 370-72).

The eternal Father is a progressive Being ... the capacity of eternal increase (Talmage, *DC*, p. 529).

JESUS CHRIST

Among the spirit children of Elohim, the first-born was and is Jehovah or Jesus Christ, to whom all others are juniors (Smith, *GD*, p. 70).

By obedience and devotion He attained to the pinnacle of intelligence which ranked him as a God, even in his pre-existent state (McConkie, *MD*, p. 192).

Jesus Christ was the executive in the work of creation, aided by Michael (or Adam), Enock, Noah, Abraham, Moses, Peter, James, John, Joseph Smith, and others (McConkie, *MD*, p. 169).

He was born of the virgin Mary. Elohim is literally the Father of the Spirit and of Jesus Christ, and also of the body (Talmage, *DC*, p. 466).

He is essentially greater than all others, by reason of His unique status in the flesh as the offspring of a mortal mother and an immortal, or resurrected and glorified Father.

He died on the cross, rose again, and is coming

again in power and glory to set up his kingdom on earth (Talmage, *DC*, p. 472).

HOLY SPIRIT

The Holy Ghost is "a personage of Spirit." He does not have a body of flesh and bones, like the Father and the Son *(DC*, 130:22).

He is "the influence of deity, the light of Christ, or of Truth" (Smith, *GD*, p. 60).

He "can only be in one place at one time" although he "emanates from Deity" like "electricity, or the universal ether ... which fills the earth and the air, and is everywhere present" (McConkie, *MD*, pp. 359, 753).

SIN

Adam fell that men might be; and men are, that they might have joy *(II Nephi*, 2:25).

Adam deliberately and wisely chose (to touch the forbidden tree) and partook of the fruit (Talmage, *DC*, p. 65).

Adam cried, "Because of my transgression my eyes are opened, and in this life I shall have joy" *(Pearl of Great Price*, Moses 5:10-11).

We ought to consider the fall of our first parents as one of the great steps to external exaltation and happiness *(Mormon Catechism)*.

We believe that men will be punished for their own sins, and not for Adam's transgression *(AF,* 2).

REDEMPTION AND SALVATION

We believe that through the atonement of Christ, all mankind may be saved, by obedience to the laws and ordinances of the gospel *(AF,* 3).

The first principles and ordinances of the gospel are: Faith on the Lord Jesus Christ; repentance; baptism by immersion for the remission of sins; and laying on of hands for the gift of the Holy Ghost *(AF,* 4).

Even the unbeliever, the heathen, and the child who dies before reaching the years of discretion, *all* are redeemed by the Savior's self-sacrifice from the individual consequences of the Fall (Talmage, p. 58).

Included are "beasts, fowls of the air, and fishes of the sea" *(DC,* 29:23-25).

The resurrection of the body (of every living thing) is one of the victories achieved by Christ through His atoning sacrifice *(Talmage,* p. 58).

They who believe not your words, and are not baptized in water in my name, for the remission of their sins … shall be damned *(DC,* 84:74).

Baptism is … the very gateway into the kingdom of heaven, an indispensable step in our salvation and exaltation (Bennet, *Why I Am a Mormon,* p. 124).

Baptism by proxy for the dead is a major

activity. "The Saints are ... redeeming their (unbaptized) dead from the grasp of Satan" (Morgan, *Plan of Salvation*, p. 8).

Celestial marriage is the gate to an exaltation in the highest heaven within the celestial world (McConkie, *MD*, p. 118).

Those who attain the highest sphere, the Celestial, will "have spirit children in the resurrection, in relation to which offspring they stand in the same position that God our Father stands to us" *(MD*, p. 257).

The second sphere, the Terrestrial, will be inhabited by "accountable persons who die without law" or who "did not accept the gospel" or with LDS who "were not valiant" *(MD*, p. 784).

RETRIBUTION

Most of the adult people who have lived since Adam (having rejected Christ and lived wickedly) will go to the "Telestial Kingdom" *(MD*, p. 784).

Perdition is for Satan, and the Sons of Perdition, angels who rebelled with him. Also for men who commit the unpardonable sin (Talmage, *DC*, p. 410).

"Endless punishment" is "God's punishment" and may endure for "one hour, one week, one year, or an age" (Morgan, *The Plan of Salvation*).

SPIRITUALISM

Spiritualism teaches that the spark of divinity dwells in all ("What Spiritualism Is and Does," *Spiritualist Manual,* 1940), however, there is no spark of divinity that dwells in all. The Holy Spirit dwells only in believers, and the Holy Spirit isn't a "spark." The trinity seems to have no adherents in advanced circles of the spirit world, and the divinity of Christ as a co-equal with the Father is universally denied. The Holy Spirit, Jesus answered and said unto him, "If a man love me, he will keep my words; and my Father will love him, and we will come unto him, and make our abode with him." (John 14:23). "But the Comforter, which is the Holy Ghost, whom the Father will send in my name, he shall teach you all things, and bring all things to your remembrance, whatsoever I have said unto you." (John 14:26) Christ is only universally denied to the unbeliever, but, to the believer, we know that he is God. "In the beginning was the Word, and the Word was with God, and the Word was God. The same was in the beginning with God. All things were made by him; and without him was not anything made that was made." (John 1:1-3) "For God so loved the world, that he gave his only begotten Son, that whosoever believeth in Him should not perish, but have everlasting life." (John 3:16)

Spiritualists have a little saying: "Just as I am, nor poor, nor blind, nor bound by chains in soul or mind for all of thee within I find, O God of Love, I come, I come." (*Spiritualistic Hymnal*) Their theory on Jesus Christ is that Christ himself was nothing more than a medium of high order. The teaching of spirits supersedes day-to-day living, instead you can go out of this realm into supernatural, an advance upon the teaching of Christianity. (*Spiritual Telegraph*, No. 37) Jesus Christ wasn't divine; He is now an advanced spirit in the sixth sphere. He never claimed to be God manifest in the flesh and does not, at present. (Weisse, *Demonology or Spiritualism*, p. 141) Jesus did not claim for himself more than he held out for others. His identification with the Father was the oneness of mediumship. He was a medium or "mediator" (Colville, *Universal Spiritualism*, p. 234) Jesus Christ was, indeed, the Son of God, as also are we sons of God. (*Many Mansions*, p. 107) Christ is now in Heaven, sitting on the right hand of the Father. "So then after the Lord had spoken unto them, He was received up into Heaven, and sat on the right hand of God." (Mark 16:19) There is no such evidence in God's Holy Word that Christ is in the sixth sphere. Again, this is a man-made thought that conflicts with the true Word of God.

Christ is God in the flesh. "I and my Father are one." (John 10:30) Christ is the mediator to man. "For there is one God, and one mediator between God and men, the man Christ Jesus." (1 Tim. 2:5) We are sons of God but not in the capacity of Jesus Christ. We are sons, through adoption, of God by the death, burial, and resurrection of Jesus Christ.

The miraculous conception of Christ is merely a fabulous tale. (Weisse, *Spiritualism*, p. 141) Spiritualists see the death of Jesus as an illustration of the martyr spirit, of that unselfish and heroic devotion to humanity which ever characterized the life of Jesus, but they see no special atoning value in his suffering and death. (*The A.B.C. of Spiritualism.* Q. 19) Spiritualism accepts him as one of many "savior Christs" who at different times have arrived in the world to lighten its darkness and show, by perception and example, the way of life to men. It recognizes him as a world savior, but not as "the only name" given under heaven by which men can be saved. (*The A.B.C. of Spiritualism*, Q, 17) Spiritualists deny the personality of the Holy Spirit. The Holy Spirit from God is the Spirit of some holy person who has once been flesh. (Hastings, p. 91) The verification of the Holy Spirit's existence can be found in the fourteenth chapter of John.

Let's answer these teachings about the Word of

God and Jesus Christ. "And they said, believe on the Lord Jesus Christ, and thou shalt be saved, and thy house." (Acts 16:31) Everyone in this particular household was saved, if anyone accept Christ Jesus as their personal savior and believe on Him they shalt be saved! "But as many as received him, to them gave he hope to become the sons of god, even to them that believe on his name." (John 1:12) Meaning anyone who comes into fellowship with Christ becomes a son or child of God. "He that believeth on him is not condemned: but he that believeth not is condemned already, because he hath not believed in the name of the only begotten Son of God." (John 3:18) Only Christ can save this world, and, if one chooses not to accept Christ as their personal savior, they will be condemned to eternal damnation. "He that believeth on the son hath everlasting life and he that believeth not the Son shall not see life; but the wrath of God abideth on him." (John 3:36) Those who don't accept Christ in their lives will suffer the wrath of god. "Not be works of righteousness which we have done, but according to his mercy he saved us, but the wasting of regeneration, and renewing of the Holy Ghost." (Titus 3:5) We are saved because of:

God's

Righteousness

Assuring

Cleansing

Expeditiously

The Holy Ghost who is God who dwells in the believer gives us the reassurance of God's Grace. "For by grace are ye saved through faith; and that not of yourselves: it is the gift of God: not of works, lest any man should boast." (Eph. 2:8-9) Again we see the word GRACE, God's Righteousness Assuring Cleansing Expeditiously. Without grace and faith the plan of salvation would not be integrated into the believer. "Being justified freely by his grace through the redemption that is in Christ Jesus." (Rom. 3:24) "For Christ is the end of the law for righteousness to every one that believeth." (Rom. 10:4) We are no longer under the law but under grace, because of the death, burial, and resurrection of Jesus Christ.

Christ is God, who came in the flesh and dwelt among men, the only begotten Son of the Father. Only

Christ can save this world from sin, only Christ can give eternal security with the Father, which is in heaven. Christ is the only one who has sacrificed His life for the world; there is no other one. We are no longer under the Old Testament laws, but of Jesus' commandment I give unto you, that you "love one another." (John 13:34) And if we follow this commandment it falls right under the Ten Commandments. These scriptures back up Christ's purpose on the earth and who he really is.

SPIRITUALISM

Spiritualism is the science, philosophy, and religion of continuous life, based upon the demonstrated fact of communication, by means of mediumship, with those who live by the spirit world.

GOD

Infinite intelligence pervades and controls the universe, is without shape or form, and is impersonal, omnipresent, and omnipotent.

It teaches that the spark of divinity dwells in all ("What Spiritualism Is and Does," *Spiritualist Manual*, 1940).

The doctrine of the trinity seems to have no adherents in advanced circles of the spirit world. The divinity of Christ as a co-equal with the Father is universally denied.

> Just as I am, nor poor, nor blind,
> Nor bound by chains in soul or mind
> For all of Thee within I find
> O God of Love, I come, I come.
> *Spiritualistic Hymnal*

JESUS CHRIST

Christ himself was nothing more than a medium of high order.

The teaching of spirits supersedes and is in advance upon the teachings of Christianity *(Spiritual Telegraph,* No. 37).

Jesus Christ was not divine. He is now an advanced spirit in the sixth sphere. He never claimed to be God manifest in the flesh and does not at present (Weisse, *Demonology or Spiritualism,* p. 141).

Jesus did not claim for himself more than he held out for others.

His identification with the Father was the oneness of mediumship. He was a medium or "mediator" (Colville, *Universal Spiritualism,* p. 234).

Jesus Christ was indeed the Son of God, as also are we sons of God *(Many Mansions,* p. 107).

The miraculous conception of Christ is merely a fabulous tale (Weisse, *Spiritualism,* p. 141).

Spiritualism sees in the death of Jesus an illustration of the martyr spirit, of that unselfish and heroic devotion to humanity which ever characterized the life of Jesus, but no special atoning value in his sufferings and death *(The A.B.C. of Spiritualism,* Q. 19).

Spiritualism accepts him as one of many Saviour Christs, who at different times have come into the world to lighten its darkness and show by precept and example the way of life to men. It recognizes him as a world Saviour but not as "the only name" given under heaven by which men can be saved *(The A.B.C. of Spiritualism,* Q. 17).

HOLY SPIRIT

Denies the personality of the Holy Spirit.

The Holy Spirit from God is the spirit of some holy person who has once been in the flesh *(Hastings,* p. 91).

SIN

Man never had a fall.

Whatever is, is right. Evil does not exist. Evil is good. No matter what man's path may be, good or bad, it is the path of divine ordination and destiny. (Childs, *Whatever Is, Is Right).*

A lie is the truth intrinsically: it holds a lawful place in creation; it is a necessity. (Andre, *The True*

Light, p. 162).

We believe in intelligent and ignorant spirits. No being is naturally bad—evil always originates in ignorance.

Death is not a violent result of sin. It was neither friend nor enemy. It is a part of the divine purpose *(SM,* 1940).

REDEMPTION

There is no atoning value in the death of Jesus Christ (Childs, *Whatever Is, Is Right).*

Salvation by vicarious atonement is a wicked and soul-destroying delusion *(Ethics of Spiritualism,* p. 99).

Teaches the continuity of life and the eternal progression of man toward perfection in the spirit realm.

That every soul will progress through the ages to heights sublime and glorious, where God is Love and Love is God ("What Spiritualism Is and Does," *SM,* 1940).

There are not worlds at all; there (is) but one interblended, interrelated world, closely interwoven by memory and the love of life. Consciousness could not die. Personality could not be destroyed (Bach, *They Have Found a Faith,* p. 116).

Life on the spirit plane is evolvement, like the

ascent in a spiral, the growth of moral affection to higher and higher "heavens."

SALVATION

We affirm the moral responsibility of the individual, and that he makes his own happiness or unhappiness as he obeys or disobeys Nature's physical and spiritual laws.

Man becomes a spirit after death, doing both evil and good, but he may be saved as he progresses from one spirit level to the next. We affirm that the doorway to reformation is never closed against any human soul, here or hereafter *(Declaration of Principles,* Nos. 7 and 8).

Leaving the physical body does not change the condition of the spirit, which is the actual personality. It must learn to desire and to progress to higher and better conditions, just as we do on earth *(SM,* p. 182).

Each must work out his own salvation; each has an equal opportunity to do this when he shall have atoned for the wrongs and overcome the temptations and allurements to the sense gratification of earth life *(SM,* p. 184).

Even the most degraded personality can in time attain the greatest heights. It is easier, however, to begin progression in the earth life *(SM,* p. 184).

RETRIBUTION

Hell does not exist and never will.

All spirit people of wisdom, knowledge, and love know there is no hell and no devil.

No resurrection—no judgment.

When you believe in spiritual manifestations, you will feel far happier than you do now. You will not fear the threats of damnation and hell ... such doctrine is wrong (Doyle, *The New Revelation,* 1918, p. 68).

We do not believe in such places as Purgatory and Hell. Communicating spirits have merely graduated from this form of life into another. That life can be heaven or hell-like, just as each spirit chooses to make it; the same applies to our life here *(SM,* p. 183).

EASTERN MYSTICISM THEOLOGY

Another denomination a Christian must consider closely is the Eastern Mysticism Theology. This theology deals with the mind and making it transparent; how to work the power of the mind to everyday life. This goes against Christian belief because Christians have God.

Eastern Mysticism views God as the Brahma, the Absolute, other than which there is nothing else— without qualities, unknowable, impersonal, beyond all appearances, changes, differences. (Walter R. Martin, *Kingdom of the Gulfs*, p. 239) Brahma, the names of God, have been listed in former sections, and Brahma isn't one of them. "Unto thee it was showed, that thou mightest know that the Lord he is God; there is none else besides him." (Deut. 4:35) Brahma isn't mentioned in the Bible. "Thou shalt have no other gods before me. Thou shalt not make unto thee any graven image, or any likeness of any thing that is in heaven above, or that is in the earth beneath, or that is in the water under the earth: Thou shalt not bow down thyself to them, nor serve them: for I the Lord thy god am a jealous God, visiting the iniquity of the fathers upon the children unto the third and fourth generation of them that hate me." (Exod. 20:3-5)

Eastern Mysticism believes that God is all there is. "All visible objects are but modifications of self-existence, of an unconscious and impersonal essence which is called God." (Walter R. Martin, *Kingdom of the Cults*, p. 239) Things exist, and people don't know it. God exists, and people don't know this; and so people exist because they make themselves exist. Because substance and matter cannot think, how do people exist if God is impersonal and unconscious and a modification of self-existence?

"In the beginning God created the heaven and the earth. And the earth was without form, and void; and darkness was upon the face of the deep. And the *Spirit of God* [the author's italics] moved upon the face of the waters." (Gen. 1:1-2) "And God said, Let us make man in our image, after our likeness; and let them have dominion over the fish of the sea, and over the fowl of the air, and over the cattle, and over the earth, and over every creeping thing that creepeth upon the earth." (Gen. 1:26) Looking at scripture we can see that God exists and that He is not an unconscious and impersonal essence which is called God. He is the Creator of all. It is he that created us, not we ourselves.

"God is not matter or substance, God is a Spirit: and they that worship Him must worship Him in Spirit and in truth." (John 4:24)

God is omnipresent and almighty, and is in the heart of everyone. (*Transcendental Meditation*, p. 61) God is the Creator of the world. The Holy Spirit dwells within people's souls. Christians believe that God isn't just in our hearts, he's everywhere. God is in the heart of his believers. Not everyone acknowledges God as the Creator, however, this is revealed by reading the false doctrines of different religious organizations.

"In his real nature, man is divine. The inner man is fully divine. Vedanta teaches no other god man but the divinity inherent in man, and his capacity for infinite evolution." (*Transcendental Meditation*, p. 61) Christians are not divine, Christ Jesus is. Man is a sinner, and if he accepts Jesus Christ as his personal Savior, he is a sinner saved by the grace of God. The Holy Spirit is divine, and he dwells inside of the believers. Transcendental Meditation deals with the mind, and the Bible doesn't back this idea up. To define Transcendental Meditation, it is the belief or doctrine that knowledge of reality is derived from intuitive sources rather than objective experience. So, therefore, with transcendental belief one will facilitate the belief by instinct without conscious reasoning.

The Eastern Mysticism theory of Jesus Christ states, "All religions from times immemorable are just different branches of the main trunk of the eternal religion represented by the Vedas." (*Transcendental*

Meditation, p. 19)

"I don't think Christ ever suffered or Christ could suffer." (*Maharishi Mahmest Yogi*, p. 123) "For even hereunto were ye called: because Christ also suffered for us, leaving us an example, that ye should follow his steps." (1 Pet. 2:21) "For Christ also hath once suffered for sins, the just for the unjust, that he might bring us to God, being put to death in the flesh, but quickened by the Spirit." (1 Pet. 3:18) These verses of scripture reveal that Christ really suffered for the whole world. Christ however, is considered to be one of a long line of "Masters" who had, themselves, realized divinity. Collectively, "they" are recognized as "divine," and are addressed as such. Through such individuals at various times in history, the "divine truth" was transmitted to men. Christ's picture is frequently to be seen beside that of Buddha, or of Shankaracharya, or Yogananda, or other recognized Divine Leaders. The "Masters" are considered to be realized expressions of divinity and, as such, are worshiped.

Christ is not from a long line of masters. Christ is the only "Master." "Ye call me Master and Lord; and ye say well; for so I am." (John 13:13) Some individuals through time thought they were masters. Buddha is a statue as well as Shankaracharya, and Yogananda. Christians worship Christ, because he's real, not because he's an idol. The Bible doesn't mention any master other than God the Father and the Lord Jesus Christ. "Neither be ye called masters, for one is your Master even Christ." (Matt. 12:10) There is no other Master or divine Father than God the Father, Christ Jesus, and the Holy Spirit who dwells inside of believers. Buddha is a statue. Shankaracharya or Yogananda are not divine leaders. These people didn't teach the true gospel of Jesus Christ. "But seek ye first the kingdom of God, and His righteousness, and all these things shall be added unto you. But seek ye first the Kingdom of God, and His righteousness, and all these things shall be added unto you." (Matt. 6:33) Seeking God first is the true way. Following man can lead you in the wrong direction. The Masters are considered to be realized expression of divinity and as such, are worshiped. "God is a Spirit, and they that worship him must worship him in spirit and in truth." (John 4:24) God is a Spirit by nature. When we worship the Lord God we are to assent to his being in spirit— meaning the things he has promised us in the heavenly realm vs. the earthly material objects—and in truth— knowing the difference between right and wrong.

Christians must keep in mind the seriousness of different errors in religious movements and these religious movements reveal how dysfunctional society is by letting man's theory and the Word of God collide to become one. Having statues as gods, having people saying that they are Christ is corrupting the world. Christians need to work together to change the theory of man and keep the true Word of God pure and untainted.

Buddhism is another religion under Eastern Mysticism. There is no absolute God in Buddhism, although many have interpreted Buddhism as a search for God. Buddhists deal with thoughts and emotions. When I was in Japan doing research on Buddhism, Zen, and Shintoism, what I found interesting was that most of the Japanese didn't know the real purpose of Buddha. All they knew was that believers pray for forgiveness and ask for help. Most of the Japanese chant their prayers. I asked one girl why she did this. She told me that she didn't know, but that her mother told her it was right so, therefore, she must obey and do the right thing. The young lady could turn to Christ, but instead she follows family values even though, in these times, people are so open. Only 2% of Japanese celebrate Christianity and understand its true meaning. Some of those who are Christians still hide because they don't fit into their own society. Christianity isn't the norm. Most Japanese don't want to have anything to do with Christianity because they feel it's an American-made theory. Because other countries or peoples feel this way, this leads to a nation that is full of lost souls. Those who worship Buddha worship a statue. Those that are Christians worship Christ. People who are of the Buddhist religion believe in reincarnation, Christians believe in life after death. Zen Buddhism believes: The major Buddhist activity solves eternity's problems by illogical Koan to produce enlightenment similar to Transcendental Meditation. We as Christians solve our problems in prayer, we receive enlightenment through God's Holy Word and by answered prayer.

Anyone who is called into the ministry as a missionary should go to a Bible college to learn the wisdom and to get the knowledge and understanding of God's Holy Word. When a person is taking on a challenge such as this, studying is the biggest key. 2 Timothy 2:15 says, "Study to show thyself approved unto God, a workman that needeth not to be ashamed, rightly dividing the Word of Truth." When people study diligently, they can decipher the difference between right and wrong teachings of false teachers. After they have studied a great deal and understand God's Holy Word, they follow Matthew 28:19-20: "Go ye therefore, and teach all nations, baptizing in the name of the Father, and of the Son, and of the Holy Ghost. Teaching them to observe all things whatsoever I have commanded you: And lo, I am with you always, even unto the end of the world. Amen." Christians can survive in a dysfunctional society by studying God's

Holy Word; they must seek him first.

Matthew 6:33 tells us: "But seek ye first the kingdom of God, and His righteousness; and all these things shall be added unto you." Christians must study very carefully so they can discern the things of this world. Jesus tells us in Matthew 24:24, "For there shall arise false Christs, and false prophets, and they shall show great signs and wonders; inasmuch that, if it were possible, they shall deceive the very elect." Some people truly know the real foundation of the Word of God, but just don't accept it as truth, and 1 John 2:18-19 reveals this: "Little children, it is the last time and as ye have heard that the Antichrist shall come, even now are there may Antichrists; whereby we know that it is the last time. They went out from us, but they were not of us. For if they had been of us, they would no doubt have continued with us, but they went out, that they might be made manifest that they were not all of us."

The two scriptures tell us that, as Christians, it takes man and his ideas along with God's Holy Word to interpret the Bible his own way. This is why the world has so many different denominations. Man feels that if issues aren't justified to his means, then he will come up with some idea to justify his goals, to justify why he is allowed to do the things that he is doing. Jesus tells us that we must be aware of these false teachers, because there are going to be many that come and try to show signs and wonders. It is so sad that people are worshiping idols like Elvis Presley. He has been dead for many years, yet he is worshiped more than Jesus Christ. Buddha, cats, and calves—one of these days worship of these things shall cease. God tells us in his commandments that there shall be no other gods before him. God is a jealous God, and when people start to worship anything, and anybody, else, this is when they are equating themselves with God.

GOD

Brahma, the Absolute, other than which there is nothing else—without qualities, unknowable, impersonal, beyond all appearances, changes, differences.

God is all there is. "All visible objects are but modifications of self-existence, of an unconscious and impersonal essence which is called God" (Walter R. Martin, *Kingdom of the Cults*, p. 239).

God is omnipresent and almighty, and is in the heart of everyone *(Transcendental Meditation,* p. 61).

In his real nature man is divine. The inner man is fully Divine. Vedanta teaches no other dogma but the divinity inherent in man, and his capacity for infinite evolution *(TM,* p. 58).

JESUS CHRIST

All religions from times immemorial are just

different branches of the main trunk of the eternal religion represented by the Vedas *(TM,* p. 19).

"I don't think Christ ever suffered or Christ could suffer" *(Maharishi Mahesh Yogi,* p. 123).

Christ is considered to be one of a long line of "Masters" who had themselves realized divinity. They are recognized as "divine," and addressed as such. Through such individuals at various times in history, the "divine truth" was transmitted to men. His picture is frequently to be seen beside that of Buddha, or of Shankaracharya, or Yogananda, or other recognized "Divine Leaders."

The "Masters" are considered to be realized expressions of divinity and, as such, are worshiped.

CURRENT RELIGIOUS MOVEMENTS FROM THE EAST

Bahaism: This emanated from Persian Islam but is essentially eclectic. All ways are of God, but Baha has the truth for this age.

Divine Light Mission: Guru Maharaj ji is presented as the Perfect Master, the Lord of the Universe, who has come to uncover the light of knowledge which is within the disciple himself.

Krishna Consciousness (Iskcon): Devotion centers on the god Krishna.

Transcendental Meditation: Deceitfully propagated as nonreligious, this is undoubtedly Hindu. Maharishi Mahesh Yogi is the leader. Mandatory initiatory rites in Sanskrit address the Lord Narayana, Brahma the Creator. Daily meditation focuses on the Source of Creative Intelligence within the individual himself.

Vedanta Society (Rama Krishna Mission): This group also teaches the Perennial Philosophy, that god is the essence of all that is, and salvation is to "realize" the god (reality) that is within you.

Yoga: This is one of the six major Hindu philosophical systems to be followed in order to obtain union (yoga) with the Ultimate, the Great All-Pervading Soul. Self-realization Fellowship advocates practice of disciplined Kriya Yoga as the path to realization of the good within, the true self.

Zen Buddhism: The major Buddhist activity solves eternity's problems by illogical Koan to produce enlightenment—similar to Transcendental Meditation.

SIN

The subject *per se* is given little attention, and forgiveness of sin is unrealistic. By the Law of Karma, "sowing and reaping," wrong actions inevitably produce punishment, good actions their reward. Salvation consists of doing good in excess of evil in order to evolve to the highest state through successive incarnations. This highest state is Enlightenment; the realization of oneness with the World-Soul, Reality.

Sin is not defined. It consists of actions which are contrary to one's "dharma" or "duty."

"Sin means wrong doing or wrong thinking due to discontentment. Suffering is the result of some wrong doing in the past."

"Past sins might induce an action in the present; some tendency of the past may come to us" *(Meditations of Mahaishi,* p. 121).

REDEMPTION AND SALVATION

"Be still and know that you are God, and when you know that you are God you will begin to live Godhood ..." (Ibid., p. 178).

Go within and experience the Divine Nature!

A mystical experience reached by various methods, which blanks out all sense impressions and releases one into a sense of identity with the great All, the only Reality!

There is no supernatural intervention. We bear the whole responsibility for our actions. If we attain the clear vision of what we are, "the Divine or Inner Light, and the god within," we need not go elsewhere. "All may say, at the moment of Awakening, 'I am the Way'" *(KC,* p. 237).

Salvation comes through the realization that

there is no duality. God is all-in-all, is all there is, and "that are Thou" *(Upanishads).*

God-realization, or Self-realization, the highest of all states of being, is a here and now possibility by any of the suggested methods. 1) The Way of Knowledge, usually involving meditation focused within. This may be aided by silent repetition of a designated, personal mantra, which is a group of sounds without meaning. Or by "Knowledge" imparted by a "master" by which "inner light" is given, and the "current of real life" (the source of life) is turned on within us. Meditation is upon this "light experience." 2) The Way of Works, following prescribed rules of conduct without desire. This is the more common way of India, much less emphasized in the West. 3) The Way of Devotion to a deity, involving continuous chanting of the chosen name, as exemplified by the vocal Krishna-Consciousness cult.

Transcendental Meditation is a path to God *(MM,* p. 59).

The way of Yoga (meaning union) is that of concentration aided by body control, with the aim being "Union with the Divine."

Self-realization is entry into the Kingdom of Heaven within, entry into the field of the Creator. "It is the gradual movement from Matter to Mind, and then to Super Mind. Once we reach the Super Mind, we reach union with the Divine."

RETRIBUTION

Heaven and hell are not accepted concepts.

Karma, the "law of the deed," of sowing and reaping, is allied with Transmigration (Reincarnation) in defining the results of sin and rewards of good.

Suffering (on earth) is the result of some wrong doing in the past, one's own repayment of deeds.

One who has attained union with God, or "God-consciousness," has reached the end of reincarnation. As the Buddha is reported to have said, "There is no rebirth for me."

ARMSTRONGISM

GOD

God is a Family, a Kingdom, not a limited trinity *(The Plain Truth,* Aug. 1958, p. 17).

The doctrine of the Trinity is false, pagan *(The Missing Dimension in Sex,* p. 37).

God is a family: God is reproducing Himself and man was created to literally become God *(What It Means to Be Equal with god,* p. 43).

At the present time there are only two beings in the God Family, 1) God the Father, Father of Jesus Christ, 2) God of Abraham, Isaac, and Jacob, the One who became Jesus Christ, God the Son *("The God Family" in Tomorrow's World,* May 1971).

You can become God ("God's Power" in *TW,* Nov. 1971, p. 12).

But quantitatively, man will never equal God the Father, just as surely as God the Creator (Jesus Christ) will Himself never quantitatively equal God the Father *(WMEG,* p. 44).

YAHWEH was the God of Israel. They (Israel) did not know God the Father ("Is Jesus God?" in *PT,* Sept. 1958).

JESUS CHRIST

BEFORE Jesus was conceived by Mary, He was not the Son of God ("Just What do You Mean—Born Again?" in *TW*, Oct. 1971, p. 43).

God the Creator (Jesus Christ) Himself will never quantitatively equal God the Father *(WMEG,* p. 45).

Jesus Christ was born a Son of God by a resurrection from the dead ... and as a born son of God, Christ is God! God Almighty His Father is God. They are two separate and individual persons *(Why Were You Born?* pp. 21-22).

God the Father did not cause Jesus Christ to get back into the body which had died. Jesus Christ was dead ... and the resurrection body was no longer human. It was Christ resurrected, immortal, once again changed *(PT,* Apr. 1963, pp. 10, 40).

Christ's body disappeared. Christ was raised as a divine spirit being *(If You Die, Will You Live Again?* p. 6).

HOLY SPIRIT

The Father and the Son are in definite locations with respect to each other ... spirit proceeds from them and fills the entire universe. Spirit is God's life *(How You Can Be Imbued with the Power of God,* p. 5).

Theologians have blindly accepted the false

doctrine that the Holy Spirit is a third person—heresy of the trinity. This limits God to Three Persons! *(Just What Do You Mean—Born Again?* pp. 17, 19).

God's Spirit dwelling in you is God's own divine love *(What Do You Mean—Unpardonable Sin?* p. 9).

Whenever we become members of God's begotten family, we receive a portion, a seed or germ, of the Father's Holy Spirit *(HYIPG,* p. 4).

Notice that the Holy Spirit, the germ by which we are begotten, comes from the Father (Ibid, p. 3).

SIN

In literally hundreds of places in your New Testament, Jesus Christ and His inspired apostles teach absolute obedience to all ten of the Ten Commandments *(PT,* Nov. 1959, p. 18).

We must repent of sin, repent of transgressing God's law, which means turning from disobedience as a prior condition to receiving God's free gift *(The Inside Story of the World Tomorrow,* p. 48).

Sickness is only the penalty of physical transgression, and whenever one is sick, he is paying that penalty. Healing is nothing more or less that the forgiveness of sin. God is the only real physician! Scripture labels other modes of healing idolatry. Medicine has a pagan origin *(Does God Heal Today?,* p. 8).

REDEMPTION

The purpose of life in us is that God is really creating His own kind, reproducing Himself. At the time of the resurrection we shall be instantaneously changed from mortal to immortal. We shall then be God! You will actually be God, even as Jesus was and is God, and His Father, a different person, also is God. You are setting out on a training to become Creator, to become God *(WWYB, pp. 21-22)*.

We ... will generate eternal life intrinsically within ourselves *(WMEG, p. 44)*.

Furthermore, we will counsel and advise our Creator-Father (Ibid., p. 45).

Physical human beings in Tomorrow's World ... will worship before the feet of God's present-day human servants *(Your Destiny—The God Family, p. 37)*.

SALVATION

Jesus alone, of all humans, has so far been saved *(WWYB, p. 11)*.

The blood of Jesus Christ does not finally save anyone. It saves merely from the death penalty (of sin) *(All About Water Baptism, pp. 1-3)*.

Baptism is an essential ordinance for salvation. You must be baptized to become a true Christian ("This is the Worldwide Church of God," in *TW*, Feb. 1971, pp. 16-17).

Along with the physical act of baptism is promised the Holy Spirit, through the laying on of hands *(TW,* Apr. 1971, pp. 41-42).

One who is born of God is merely begotten spiritually. He is not yet really born. Only those who develop spirituality shall finally be given immortality … at the second coming of Christ *(AAWB,* p. 2).

When Jesus Christ returns to this earth, He will, for the first time, set His hand to save the world. He will offer salvation (to all people) *(There Is a Real Hell Fire,* p. 6).

A majority of those who die without Christ will be resurrected and gain opportunity to believe during the Millennium *(Predestination—Does the Bible Teach It?).*

RETRIBUTION

When a human being dies, he is DEAD, which means that his body, mind, and soul are all dead. He simply stops being *(Do You Have an Immortal Soul?* p. 41).

The wicked will be resurrected at the close of the Millennium, but only to be annihilated *(Lazarus and the Rich Man).*

Rebellion against the Law of God means eternal punishment and everlasting death. God will save no person He does not rule *(Which Day Is the Christian*

Sabbath? pp. 35, 58, 93, 94).

"Everlasting" means "age-ending." The translation "everlasting" is misleading, since the fire itself will not burn forever.

The concept of "hell" is part and parcel of the folklore and mythology of the whole world ... as a place of punishment and torture of the wicked *(TW,* pp. 14, 18).

THE WAY INTERNATIONAL

GOD

Elohim, God alone, is Creator of heaven and earth. The Bible teaches that there is only one true God, that God was in Christ, that God is Spirit, and that God is eternal whereas Jesus was born (Wierwille, *The Word's Way,* p. 26).

God is most holy; God has no equal. God alone holds the power of salvation (Wierwille, *Jesus Christ Is Not God,* p. 124).

The Trinitarian dogma degrades God from His elevated, unparalleled position. Besides, it leaves man unredeemed *(JC,* book jacket).

Biblically there are three: 1) God who is the Holy Spirit, the Father of our Lord Jesus Christ, 2) Jesus Christ, the Son of God and the son of man, and 3) the holy spirit, God's gift, which God made available on the day of Pentecost *(JC,* p. 123).

JESUS CHRIST

The gospel of John established the truth of God's word that Jesus Christ was the Son of God, but not God the Son—or God Himself *(JC,* p. 16).

Jesus Christ's existence began when he was

conceived by God creating the soul-life of Jesus in Mary *(WW,* p. 37).

The created word (Jesus Christ) was with God in His foreknowledge—the same way that "we the chosen of God" were called in Him in His foreknowledge *(JC,* p. 85).

When Jesus was born, he came into existence … Foreknowledge became a reality (JC, p. 85).

Jesus and God are not one from the beginning, but they were one in purpose *(JC,* pp. 119-20).

Jesus just "took part, not all" of Adam's flesh and blood *(JC,* p. 71).

He was sinless because he was conceived by the Holy Spirit, yet was born of Mary with a body of flesh, as all mankind *(WW,* p. 161).

Jesus Christ was a man … whose life was without blemish and without spot, a lamb from the flock, thereby being the perfect sacrifice. Thus he became our redeemer *(JC,* p. 79).

After Jesus Christ was sacrificed, was resurrected and then ascended, it was possible for God to send His gift which dwells permanently in all believers *(JC,* p. 133).

HOLY SPIRIT

God is holy, and God is Spirit. The gift that He gives is holy spirit *(JC,* pp. 27-28).

Many confuse the Giver, Holy Spirit, with the gift, holy spirit *(JC,* p. 128).

In the new birth, man receives spirit from God, who is the Spirit *(JC,* p. 128).

The speaking in tongues was the external manifestation of the receiving of the gift of holy spirit *(JC,* p. 131).

At Pentecost the speaking in tongues was the external manifestation of the receiving of the gift of holy spirit ... At the conclusion of his (Peter's) message, he taught them how to receive the new birth and speak in tongues *(JC,* p. 131).

The holy spirit field ... is the field God raised me up for ... There's no one I can't lead into speaking in tongues, if they are Christian and want to do it (Elena S. Whiteside, *The Way—Living in Love,* p. 178).

To worship by the spirit we must operate a manifestation of the holy spirit ... which produces true worship in speaking in tongues (Wierwille, *The New, Dynamic Church,* p. 90).

MAN AND SIN

We, as well as Jesus Christ, were with God in His foreknowledge, but not in existence, before the foundation of the world *(JC,* p. 29).

The Bible teaches that all men since Adam are born "dead in trespasses and sin" *(JC,* p. 70).

When Adam sinned, Satan, who was the supreme enemy of God, obtained absolute control over all that which God had originally given to Adam *(NDC,* p. 59).

What does God see on the palms of our hands? He sees on them nothing but sin, doubt, fear, bitterness, quarrels, lies, hatred—everything that stains a sinner (Wierwille, *The Bible Tells Me So,* p. 108).

Man fell because of disobedience to God's Word *(JC,* p. 66).

The spirit departed from Adam ... Adam and Eve's spiritual connection with God was lost *(JC,* p. 67).

REDEMPTION AND SALVATION

The Bible clearly teaches that Jesus Christ was a man conceived by the Holy Spirit, God, whose life was without blemish and without spot, a lamb from the flock, thereby being the perfect sacrifice. Thus he became our redeemer *(JC,* p. 79).

Jesus brought righteousness because he willingly gave himself as a perfect, sinless sacrifice, a perfect redeemer *(JC,* p. 76).

There are two parts: sin and disease, one is removed by the blood of the lamb and the other by the flesh of the lamb *(BT,* p. 87).

Christ has redeemed us, not only from some of the things mentioned in the curse, but from all of them, which includes sickness and disease *(BT,* p. 84).

... the physical punishment which he went through ... brought our healing *(BT,* p. 84).

When we have salvation, we have wholeness, even physical wholeness, if we simply accept it *(NDC,* p. 310).

God is our Savior as the author of the plan of salvation. Jesus Christ made the new birth available as the agent of the plan of salvation and as the finisher of faith *(JC,* p. 147).

All born-again believers have "the faith of Jesus Christ" which is the measure given to EVERYONE when he believes. After a person has confessed with his mouth the Lord Jesus and has believed in his heart that God raised Jesus from the dead, he is a privileged son of God with access to all His promises *(NDC,* p. 29).

... you are made alive spiritually but also your physical body is made alive even now *(NDC,* p. 33).

NOTE: The church of Israel, which is the bride of Christ ... is the church of the period of the Law and of the gospels ... also the church of the Revelation. The body of Christ began on the Day of Pentecost and continues until the return of Christ. Everyone who is born again by God's Spirit is a member of the Church of Grace, the body of Christ *(NDC,* pp. 7, 10).

RETRIBUTION

The result of the one man's work (Adam's) was death; the result of the other was life *(JC,* p. 75).

Man's freedom of will permits him to choose the seed he wants and thus determine his own destiny ... One who accepts the seed of God the father of our Lord Jesus Christ has his seed eternally ... When a person accepts the seed of the devil, he has it eternally ... One seed means eternal life; the other, eternal damnation *(WW,* p. 70).

Death for the believer is referred to as falling asleep because in sleep there is an awakening point. But for the unbeliever, the Christ rejector, the ungodly, their resurrection is temporary for they shall meet a second and final death (Wierwille, *Are the Dead Alive Now?,* p. 98).

WORD OF GOD

PERSONALITY OF THE GODHEAD

In the beginning God created the heaven and the earth (Genesis 1:1).

He is God; there is none else beside him (Deuteronomy 4:35).

God is a Spirit; and they that worship him must worship him in spirit and in truth (John 4:24).

For there is one God, and one mediator between God and men, the man, Christ Jesus (1 Timothy 2:5).

Go ... and teach all nations, baptizing them in the name of the Father, and of the Son, and of the Holy Spirit (Matthew 28:19).

Jesus was baptized; the Spirit descended; the Father spoke (Matthew 3:16-17).

Come let us go down, and there confound their language, that they may not understand one another's speech (Genesis 11:7).

From the time that it was, there am I; and now the Lord God, and his Spirit, hath sent me (Isaiah 48:16).

JESUS CHRIST

In the beginning was the Word, ... and the Word

was God (John 1:1).

When, as His mother, Mary, was espoused to Joseph, before they came together, she was found with child of the Holy Spirit (Matthew 1:18).

Behold, the virgin shall conceive, and bear a son, and shall call his name Immanuel (Isaiah 7:14).

God was manifest in the flesh, justified in the Spirit, seen of angels, preached unto the nations, believed on in the world, received up into glory (1 Timothy 3:16).

And the Word was made flesh, and dwelt among us (and we beheld his glory, the glory as of the only begotten of the Father), full of grace and truth (John 1:14).

No man hath seen God at any time; the only begotten Son, who is in the bosom of the Father, he hath declared him (John 1:18).

And declared to be the Son of God with power, according to the spirit of holiness, by the resurrection from the dead (Roman 1:4).

And if Christ be not raised, your faith is vain (1 Corinthians 15:17).

Wherefore, he is able also to save them to the uttermost that come unto God by him, seeing he ever liveth to make intercession for them (Hebrew 7:25).
This same Jesus ... shall so come in like manner as ye have seen him go into Heaven (Acts 1:11; cf. John 14:3;

1 Thessalonians 4:13-18).

HOLY SPIRIT

When the Comforter is come, whom I will send unto you from the Father, even the Spirit of truth, ... he shall testify of me (John 15:26).

When he is come, he will reprove the world of sin, and of righteousness, and of judgment (John 16:8).

When he, the Spirit of truth, is come, he will guide you into all truth (John 16:13).

The Comforter, who is the Holy Spirit, ... he shall teach you all things (John 14:26).

His spirit that dwelleth in you (Romans 8:11).

Be filled with the Spirit (Ephesians 5:18; see also 1 Corinthians 3:16; Ephesians 3:16).

But ye are not in the flesh but in the Spirit, if so be that the Spirit of God dwell in you. Now if any man have not the Spirit of Christ, he is none of his (Romans 8:9; see also vv. 14, 16).

SIN

There is none righteous, no, not one (Romans 3:10).

For all have sinned, and come short of the glory of God (Romans 3:23).

If we say that we have not sinned, we make him a liar, and his word is not in us (1 John 1:10).

If we say that we have no sin, we deceive ourselves, and the truth is not in us (1 John 1:8).

Whosoever committeth sin transgresseth also the law; for sin is the transgression of the law (1 John 3:3).

All unrighteousness is sin, and there is a sin not unto death (1 John 5:17).

Whatever is not of faith is sin (Romans 14:23).

Therefore, to him that knoweth to do good, and doeth it not, to him it is sin (James 4:17).

REDEMPTION

We have redemption through his blood, the forgiveness of sins (Ephesians 1:7).

Ye were not redeemed with corruptible things … but with the precious blood of Christ (1 Peter 1:18-19).

Unto him that loveth us, and washed us from our sins in his own blood, and hath made us a kingdom of priests unto God and his father (Revelation 1:5-6).

Without shedding of blood is no remission (Hebrews 9:22).

Made peace through the blood of his cross (Colossians 1:20).

This man, after he had offered one sacrifice for sins forever, sat down on the right hand of God … For by one offering he hath perfected forever them that are sanctified (Hebrews 10:12, 14).

SALVATION

Believe on the Lord Jesus Christ, and thou shalt be saved, and thy house (Acts 16:31).

But as many as received him, to them gave he power to become the children of God, even to them that believe on his name (John 1:12).

He that believeth on him is not condemned; but he that believeth not is condemned already, because he hath not believed in the ... only begotten Son of God (John 3:18).

He that believeth on the Son hath everlasting life; and he that believeth not the Son shall not see life (John 3:36).

Not by works of righteousness which we have done, but according to his mercy he saved us, by the washing of regeneration, and renewing of the Holy Spirit (Titus 3:5).

For by grace are ye saved through faith; and that not of yourselves, it is the gift of God—not of works, lest any man should boast (Ephesians 2:8-9).

Justified freely ... through the redemption that is in Christ Jesus (Romans 3:24).

Christ is the end of the law for righteousness to everyone that believeth (Romans 10:4).

RETRIBUTION

The wages of sin is death (Romans 6:23).

Those who sleep in the dust ... shall awake, some to everlasting life, and some to shame, and everlasting contempt (Daniel 12:2).

And as it is appointed unto men once to die, but after this the judgment (Hebrews 9:27).

And I saw the dead, small and great, stand before God ... And the dead were judged out of those things ... written in the books, according to their works (Revelation 20:12).

The Lord Jesus shall be revealed from heaven ... in flaming fire taking vengeance on them that know not God, and that obey not the gospel ...; who shall be punished with everlasting destruction (2 Thessalonians 1:7-10).

If thy foot offend thee, cut it off; it is better for thee to enter lame into life than, having two feet, to be cast into hell, into the fire that never shall be quenched (Mark 9:45).

1 Corinthians 15:1-4 states, "Moreover, brethren, I declare unto you the gospel which I preached unto you, which also ye have received and wherever ye stand. By which also ye are saved, if ye keep in memory what I preached unto you, unless ye have believed in vain. For I delivered unto you first of all that which I also received how hath Christ died for our sins according to the scriptures and that He was buried, and that he rose again the third day according to the scriptures." Anytime a Christian comes across someone who is mocking the Word of God, they should preach the true Gospel of Jesus Christ, following the five steps a Christian must keep in mind while preaching against dysfunctional religions:

The first step:

The Gospel must be preached. Mark 16:15 states, "Go ye into the world and preach the gospel to every creature.

The second step:

The Gospel must be received. John 1:12 says, "But as many as received Him, to them gave He power to become the Sons of god, even to them that believe on His name."

The third step:

The Gospel must be obeyed. Romans 1:5 says, "By whom we have received grace and apostleship, for obedience to the faith among all nations, for His name."

The fourth step:

The main point of the Gospel of Christ is salvation; the death of Christ. Hebrews 9:15 says, "For this cause He is the mediator of the new testament, that by means of death, for the redemption of the transgressions that were under the first testament, they which are called might receive the promise of eternal inheritance." The burial of Christ. John 12:7 says, "let her alone; against the day of my burying hath she kept this." The Resurrection of Christ. 2 Corinthians 5:15: "And that He died for all, that they which live should not henceforth live unto themselves, but unto Him which died for them and rose again."

One trait of those who mock the Word of God is that they keep their Bible in their left hand—their book is their authority. Those who mock the Word of God feel they are the only saved people. Romans 14:10 says, "But why dost thou judge thy brother? Or why dost thou set at naught thy brother? For we shall all stand before the judgment seat of Christ." (Rev. 3:14)

Another trait is that those who mock the Word

of God use their own literature more than the Word of God. Like the Jehovah's Witnesses use the *Watch Tower*, the Mormons use the *Book of Mormon*, the Muslims use the *Koran*, the Unification Church uses the Bible and the Unity Church uses the Bible. The Bible says all scripture is given by inspiration of God, and is profitable for doctrine, for reproof, for correction, for instruction in righteousness. "The man of God may be perfect, thoroughly furnished unto all good work." (2 Tim. 3:16-17)

Only Christ can judge man, not man themselves and these are key points of a cult. If a religion doesn't teach the death, burial, and resurrection of Jesus Christ and that He is the Son of the Living God, it is a dysfunctional religion. If the religion teaches that its members are the only saved people, then it is also a cult.

As we look at why the Word of God is a mockery to the dysfunctional society, we touch on issues and beliefs on different doctrine such as Jehovah's Witnesses, Christian Science, Spiritualism, Armstrongism, Mormonism, Eastern Mysticism, The Way International, Unity, Unification Church. Let us see how these doctrine differ from the Word of God.

FOOTNOTES

PERSONALITY OF THE GODHEAD
Cross References to Genesis 1:1:
Job 38:4; Psalm 102:25; Isa. 48:13; John 1:1; Ps. 89:11; Ps. 90:2; Acts 17:24; Prov. 3:19; Isa. 42:5

Cross References to Deuteronomy 4:35:
Deut. 4:39; Exod. 8:10; Mark 12:32

Cross References to 1 Timothy 2:5:
Rom. 3:30; Gal. 3:20; Matt. 1:1

Cross References to Matthew 28:19:
Mark 16:15; Matt. 13:52; Acts 14:21; Luke 24 :47; Matt. 25:32; Acts 2:38, 8:16; Rom. 6:3; 1 Cor. 1:13-17; Gal. 3:27

Cross References to Matthew 3:16-17:
John 1:32; Matt 12:18, 17:5; Mark 9:7; Luke 9:35; Isa. 42:1

Cross References to Gen 11:7:
Gen. 1:26; Exod. 4:11; Isa. 33:19

Cross References to Isaiah 48:16:
Isa. 34:1, 41:1, 57:3; Isa. 45:19; Isa. 43:13.

JESUS CHRIST

Cross References to John 1:1:
Gen. 1:1; Col. 1:17; 1 John 1:1; John 1:14; Rev. 19:13; 1 John 1:2; John 17:5; Phil. 2:6

Cross Reference Matthew 1:18:
Luke 1:27; Matt. 12:46; Luke 1:35

Cross References to 1 Timothy 3:16:
Rom. 16:25; John 1:14; Rom. 3:4; Luke 2:13; Rom. 16:26; 2 Thes. 1:10; Acts 1:9

Cross References to John 1:14:
Rev. 19:13; Rom. 1:3; Gal. 4:4; Heb. 2:14; Rev. 21:3; Luke 9:32; John 2:11; 1 John 1:1; John 1:17; Rom. 5:21; John 8:32; John 14:6; John 18:37

Cross References to John 1:18:
Exod. 33:20; John 6:46; Col. 1:15; John 3:16,18; 1 John 4:9; John 13:23; Luke 16:22; John 3:11

Cross References to Romans 1:4:
Matt. 4:3

Cross References to I Corinthians 15:17:
Rom. 4:25

Cross References to Hebrews 7:25:
1 Col. 1:21; Heb. 7:19; Rom. 8:34

Cross Reference to Acts 1:11, John 14:3, 1 Thes. 4:13-18:
Acts 2:7; Acts 13:31; Matt. 16:27; Acts 3:21; Ezec. 14:4; John 14:18,28; John 12:26; Rom. 1:13; Acts 7:40; 1 Thes. 5:6; Eph. 2:2; 1 Col. 154:18; 1 Thes. 3:13; 1 Kings 13:17; Gal. 1:12; 1 Col. 15:52; 1 Thes. 2:19; 1 Col. 15:18

HOLY SPIRIT

Cross References to John 16:13:
John 14:17, 14:26; Acts 1:1

Cross References to John 14:26:
John 14:16, 1:33, 15:26, 16:7, 16:13; 1 John 2:20; John 2:22

Cross References to Romans 8:11:
Acts 2:24; Rom. 6:4; John 5:21; Rom. 8:1; Rom. 16:3

Cross References to Ephesians 5:18:
Prov. 20:1, 23:31; Titus 1:6; Luke 1:15
Cross References to I Cor 3:16:
Rom. 6:16; 1 Col. 6:19; Eph. 2:21

Cross References to Eph 3:16:
Eph. 3:8; Phil. 4:3; Rom. 7:22

Cross References to Romans 8:9, 14,16:
Rom. 7:5, 8:11; 1 Col. 3:16; John 14:23; Gal. 4:6; Phil. 1:19; John 14:17; Gal. 5:18; John 1:12; 2 Col. 6:18; Gal. 3:26; Acts 5:32; Rom. 8:14

The true religion is the Gospel of Jesus Christ. No Vedas, no Buddha, no Guru Maharaja, no Koon, no Mary Bakker Eddy, no Joseph Smith, no Charles Russel, no Shankaracharya, or Yogananda. These people and statues are not gods nor masters. The true religion is the death, burial and resurrection of Jesus Christ. These people did teach this false doctrine.

HOW DO YOU KNOW WHEN YOU HAVE THE RIGHT LEADER IN THE RIGHT POSITION WITHOUT CHRISTIANITY?

Since politics plays a part in today's society, how does politics play a part in God's house? Many people are turning God's house into a political house. By using "political tactics" people are maneuvering within a group to expedite goals that they are trying to achieve. People aren't going to church to worship God, but are going for prestige, compliments, and economic resources. How does Jesus feel about this? "And Jesus went into the temple of God, and cast out all them that sold and bought in the temple and overthrew the tables of the moneychangers and the seats of them that sold doves, and said unto them, 'It is written, My house shall be called the house of prayer; but ye have made it a den of thieves.'" (Matt. 21:12-13). One must also look at the next verse. "And the blind and the lame came to him in the temple; and he healed them."

God's house is a House of Prayer, giving, and thanksgiving, not for playing and entertainment; but this is the direction the church is going. In today's society, people are putting themselves in positions that aren't suitable. The Bible says, "Let your light so shine before men, that they may see your good works and glorify your Father which is in heaven." (Matt. 5:16) When it comes to "worldly positions," a light may shine, but is not of God, it is of man.

When looking for someone to lead, a person who is called by God should offer compelling evidence that he or she has the relationship, vision, and caring for people that will allow them to lead a church or group effectively. The Bible says, "Now there are diversities of gifts, by the same Spirit." (1 Cor. 12:4) "But the manifestation of the Spirit is given to every man to profit withal. For to one is given by the Spirit the word of wisdom; to another the word of knowledge by the same spirit; to another forth by the same spirit; to another the gifts of healing by the same spirit; to another the working of miracles; to another prophecy; to another discerning of spirits, to another diverse kinds of tongues; to another the interpretation of tongues: But all these worketh that one and the selfsame spirit, dividing to every man severally as he will." (1 Cor. 12:7-11)

Charles Ryrie, a twentieth century Biblical scholar at Dallas Theological Seminary, breaks down these interpretations of the Spirit gifts; the word of wisdom, the communication of spiritual wisdom; the word of knowledge, the communication of practical truth; faith, unusual reliance on God; Gifts of healing included restoration of life. Acts 9:40 and 20:12 originates this list. Prophecy is the ability to proclaim new revelation from God. Tongues and interpretation of tongues is the ability to speak and interpret languages unknown to the speaker or the interpreter. Discerning of spirits is being able to cipher the difference between right and wrong. It's very crucial for society to examining these spiritual gifts. If society does not, the world's practical standards will go below the morality level, and this will bring the world to a level where nothing really matters.

Ephesians 4:11-13 states: "And he gave some, Apostles; and some, Prophets; and some, pastors and teachers; for the perfecting of the saints, for the work of the ministry, for the edifying of the body of Christ." Until all people unify in faith and of the knowledge of the Son of God, unto a perfect man, unto the measures of the stature of the fullness of Christ. They will understand how to fulfill the standards of Christ and to be able to fight against all odds that prevail against them.

The word apostle in the previously quoted scripture means one sent forth as an ambassador who bears a message and who represents the one who sent him. Modern day leaders such as pastors, bishops, elders, and deacons do not fit the qualifications of the apostles, but they also have their own qualifications. The qualifications to be an apostle include:

1) Seeing the Lord and being an eyewitness to His (Christ's) resurrections. (Acts 1:3)

2) Being invested with miraculous signs— gifts—to confirm their message from Christ. (Acts 2:1-4)

3) Being chosen by the Lord Jesus. (Matt. 10:1-5)

Both apostles and prophets, strictly speaking, were those who were given direct revelations by God to communicate to men. Evangelists are preachers of the gospel. Pastors' and teachers' ministries are correlated here, but the directive of pastors and bishops, deacons and elders are as follows:

1) Must be the husband of one wife (1 Tim. 3:2)
2) Vigilant (1 Tim. 3:2)
3) Sober (1 Tim. 3:2)
4) Of good behavior (1 Tim. 3:2)
5) Given to hospitality (1 Tim. 3:2)
6) Apt to teach (1 Tim. 3:2).
7) Not given to wine (1 Tim. 3:3)
8) No striker (1 Tim. 3:3)
9) Not greedy of filthy lucre (1 Tim. 3:3)
10) But patient, not a brawler (1 Tim. 3:3)
11) Not covetous (1 Tim. 3:3)
12) One that ruleth well his own house (1 Tim. 3:4)
13) Having his children in subjection with all gravity (1 Tim. 3:4)
14) Not a novice, lest being lifted up with pride he fall into the condemnation of the devil (1 Tim. 3:6)
15) Moreover, he must have a good report of them which are without; lest he fall into

reproach and the snare of the devil (1 Tim. 3:7)

The purpose of these directives from 1 Timothy is to let society know that the words of God in the Holy Bible are put there for reasons and purposes and not for mockery and show-and-tell. People should follow these rules for Godly order and not for "political tactics" to gain any recognition within a church or Christian organization. "That we henceforth be no more children, tossed to and fro, and carried about with every wind of doctrine by the sleight of men, and cunning craftiness, whereby they lie in wait to deceive." (Eph. 4:14) Being educated in the Word of the Lord will help the children of God know what is coming upon them. When looking for an individual to fit in God's service, after looking at all these gifts, the scripture's standard states the best outward reputation. A leader must:

1) Have a good reputation even when his life is lived as an open book (1 Tim. 3:2; Titus 1:7)
2) Be well thought of, even by those outside the church (1 Tim. 3:7)
3) Be irreproachable in his marital relations (1 Tim. 3:2; Titus 1:6)

In other words, a pastor is to be a man who has a good reputation in his church, in society, and in his home. (Matt. 5:6)

Robert W. Dingman is an Executive Search Consultant, he has established his own consulting firm. He's been helping churches find the right leaders for their congregation for the past twenty-five years. He shows us how important it is to inquire about a Christian's leadership ability. Mr. Dingman's book, *The Complete Search Committee Guide Book*, makes a point that the people whom are looking to be leaders must be well liked by other pastors or Biblical committees. The church is a divine institution founded by Christ and the apostles, and it has done more to purify, enrich, and strengthen mankind than have all other movements. It's still the most powerful and beneficent establishment for promoting morality and religion. If the church is to grow, so as to meet the growing needs of the age, it must have able men and women in its ministry. Without such leadership, there is a danger that the Church will ultimately be reduced to a negligible force. The failure to raise up a competent ministry would be a far greater failure than not to bring converts to the Christian faith, because the enlarging of the kingdom waits for leaders of power. What problems of the church exist today which cannot best be solved by enlisting for the best leadership, calling more men of the highest qualifications? What calamity, next to the withdrawal of Christ's presence, should be more dreaded than to have young men of genius, and of large equipment, withhold themselves from responding to the call of the Christian ministry? Yet, this is the calamity which is impending. (Lightfoot, J.B., *The Christian Ministry*, p. 2)

Where does politics play a great part in God's house? It doesn't. If the church places people into leadership roles who aren't qualified, the church will die, the people will stay lost, and there will be no growth. The need for the gifts detailed previously is to delegate what should stay and what should go. Education and experience is very important, because people look over these important matters in finding quality people to play a great part in God's house.

As the progress of the Christian religion is of the most fundamental and vital interest, it must not be committed to the charge of incompetent hands. Men of ability should be in God's position; i.e., men of personal force or strength of personality. Men of sound physical constitution who have the requisite common sense and self-control to care for the body should be placed in important positions, thus ensuring its best working efficiency. Men of mental power and proper habits of study, determined not to stagnate intellectually, should also be placed in important positions. They should have the ability to appreciate and the will to employ the best methods of study, and that is more important than the most coveted university degrees. They should be men

possessing the ability to express sympathy and friendship, and they should have a genuine religious experience. Ministers who don't know Christ first hand, who
don't have a clear and vital faith, cannot speak with the
tone of authority that should characterize the pulpit.
They must have a message and the consciousness of a
mission. They should be able to give effective expression to their passion for Christ and for men. They
should be men of intensely moral enthusiasm. Men
with hearts aflame with the passion of the cross and
ready to stake everything on their cause will succeed.
(Mott, John R., *The Future Leadership of the Church*,
p. 11) The modern ministry requires men of heroic
spirit like Knox, a twentieth century pastor, on whose
grave it reads, "Here lies one who never feared the face
of man."

George A. Gordon, pastor of the Old South
Church of Boston, Massachusetts, and author of "The
Claims of the Ministry Upon Strong Men" in *The
Ministry as a Profession* lists some of the steps that
makes and effective leader:

1) They should also be able to organize, lead,
   and inspire others to work. The growing lay
   forces of the churches need to be marshaled
   and guided. Above all, ministers should be
   great in character—men whose lives are
   modeled upon the life of Christ and are

yielded unreservedly to his way. "The only profession which consists in being something," said President Woodrow Wilson with fine insight, "is the ministry of our Lord and Savior—and it does not consist of anything else. It is manifested in other things, but it does not consist of anything else."

2) The world is losing respect for the ministers, and this age has produced a new viewpoint. The minister is respected not because he is a minister, but because he is a man who answers to the test required of the Church.

3) "If our religion is to be great and to do great things, it must be in the care of great souls— souls great in illumination and in intense and pure desire."

FOOTNOTES:

1) Taken from James Stalker, *John Knox: His Ideas and Ideals,* p. 94.

2) From an address at a conference of students of eastern colleges, held at Hartford Theological Seminary in April, 1906.

3) George A. Gordon, "The Claims of the Ministry Upon Strong Men" in *The Ministry as a Profession.* (Addresses delivered before the Divinity Club of the Harvard Divinity School. p. 6, 1906).

There are a lot of people who would use God's works for their own personal gain. They will knock down God's people to get whatever they want. In God's church, there are a lot of people in positions others want, and the church is falling apart. People are afraid to hear the truth about what they really need. How can you tell, then, if a person is in the right position of leadership—by the fruit that they bear. What I'm saying about politics is that the church, which is God's property, doesn't belong to man. It is not man's job to put anyone in a position based on prestige and character-building in a church or Christian organization. It is man's job to listen to God in order to make the right decision. Politics does not belong in God's house, it takes away the foundation of a God-center formation. If you ask me, again, how do you know when you have the right leader in the right position? The answer is, "Without Christianity is just won't work!"

WHY MUST A CHRISTIAN SUFFER WHEN IT COMES TO EARTHLY MATERIALS?

Lord, why must a Christian suffer? Why can't Christians have earthly materials? Lord, is it us or just our imagination?

It seems that every time a Christian looks around, those who don't serve God seem to get more than those who seek God. Christians are on their knees praying, fasting for strength, asking for power, and they don't get anything. When a Christian suffers they can't help but look at themselves, because the people of the world have great cars, houses, jobs, and chances to travel. Those who serve God get headaches and jobs that are stressful. Some Christians live in houses that are barely standing and have problems such as having their heating systems or their electricity turned off, or even having their telephone disconnected: they barely have any food on their tables and clothes on their backs. But they continue to serve and seek God. As a Christian, one sees all of the world's luxuries and wonders, "Why can't I have these things?"

God lets us know that he takes care of his own. Psalms 37:1 states: "Fret not thyself because of evil-doers, neither be thou envious against the workers of iniquity." Psalms 37:7 says, "Rest in the Lord, and wait patiently for Him: Fret not thyself because of the man who bringeth wicked devices to pass." Also, Psalms 37:4 goes on to say: "Delight thyself also in the Lord; and he shall give thee the desires of thine heart." God also lets us know in Psalms 37:16 that a little that a righteous man has is better than the riches of many wicked.

David, the author of the book of Psalms wrote, "I have been young, and now am old; yet have I not seen the righteous forsaken nor his seed begging bread." (Psalms 37:25) Author Spiros Zodheates, Th.D., a twentieth century Biblical scholar, explains that David, personally, had never seen "the righteous forsaken nor his seed begging bread." This doesn't mean that this never occurs; God does take care of his people. There is enough wealth in the world to provide food, clothing, and shelter for all, however, some do get more than their share while others suffer. If a good man is wasteful, acts unwisely, or speculates unduly, then God won't intervene to keep him from ruin. Jesus states in Matthew 6:25-26; "Therefore I say unto you, take no thought for your life, what ye shall eat, or what ye shall drink; nor yet for your body, what ye shall put on. Is not the life more than meat, and the body than raiment? Behold the fowls of the air: for they sow not, neither do they reap, nor gather into barns; yet your heavenly Father feedeth them. Are ye not much better than they?" Right here Christ lets us know that we are not to be anxious, and 1 John 2:15-17 further explains; "Love not the world, neither the things that are in the world. If any man love the world, the love of the Father is not in him. For all that is in the world, the lust of the flesh, and the lust of the eyes, and the pride of life is not of the Father, but is of the world. And the world passeth away, and the lust thereof: but he that doeth the will of God abideth forever." Reading these scriptures gives a Christian comfort to know that their Heavenly Father takes good care of his children. These scriptures also reveal to us what material goods mean to God.

Remember Job. Job was a man who loved God and did everything God commanded him to do. One day Job's life went downhill, and he couldn't understand why. He lost his children, his fortune, his cattle, and everything that he had. Why did this happen to Job? Because God wanted Job to know that he is God and that he has everything in control. Daniel Liderback is a twentieth century Biblical scholar. Liderback's book, *Why Do We Suffer*, says, "Job is the mirror image of each human. Like each of us, Job is confronted by an unexpected suffering, but is left without any comprehension about why he suffers. As for us, so for Job, suffering remains always incomprehensible." (p. 4)

Even though God allowed Satan to make Job suffer, God wanted Job to know he has the power to rule and control all. Job's suffering allowed him, as a person, to grow in the fellowship with God, and his faith only increased through his suffering.

Another reason a person feels he or she suffers

is because they have sinned. Daniel Liderback also states "Job does illumine one facet of suffering for us. He insisted that suffering cannot be caused by sin. Thus, he summoned us to liberate ourselves from the self-induced guilt which assumes that we suffer because we have sinned." (p. 4)

Author Gustavo Gutierrez, a twentieth century theologian and professor of theology at the Catholic University says in his book, *Job, God—Talk and the Suffering of the Innocent*, "It is important that we be clear from the outset that the theme of the book of Job is not precisely on suffering, that impenetrable human mystery, but rather how to speak of God in the midst of suffering." (p. 13) During all of Job's suffering, Job knew God was in control. Gustavo Gutierrez gives this answer, "But if human beings cannot be condemned in order to defend God, neither can God be condemned in order to defend human beings. Job learns this gradually. In the process he will become a believer who possesses the peace to which the contemplation of God ultimately leads him." Sometimes, we as Christians, must be quiet and stand still and listen, to think of the goodness of God during the midst of our suffering. Think if God would have not created the world where we be. Job always knew that God was in control, but he wanted to know whether God cared even though he was in the midst of suffering.

Professor Dan Dyke a twentieth century Old Testament professor at Cincinnati Bible College answers the question, "Why does a Christian suffer," or "Why did Job suffer," by saying that God wanted Job and Christians to know that God controls the Heavens and the Earth. Frederich Sontag's book, *God, Why Did You Do That?*, gives the answer as, "Because I wanted to!" Sontag, an instructor of Theology at Union Theological Seminary also asks, "Why did he choose to do it in just this way?" The answer to this question is, "Because I wanted to!" A fitting reply for God to make!

What we as Christians fail to see is that only God, not man, is really beyond good and evil. Humans' value structure has a certain flexibility and a certain looseness that enables them to substitute one form of value for another, but, on the whole, its form can only be radically altered as thought more than as fact. Man can follow God's freedom to form different basic sets of values, but, given his decision for this world, man's range is set on good and evil and not above it. Again, why must a Christian suffer to stay humble and to know that God is God!

Pierre Terlhard de Chardin is a philosopher and a Jesuit Priest. In his book, *On Suffering* (M'enelsure—Saulz, 23 November 1916), he states "And I have come to think that the only, the supreme, prayer we can offer up, during these hours when the road before us is shrouded in darkness, is that of our Master on the cross: *In Manus tuas Commendo Spiritum Meum!* to the hands that broke and gave life to the bread, that blesses and caressed, that were pierced; to the kindly and misty hands that reached down to the very marrow of the soul … that mold and create … to the hands through which so great a love is transmitted. It is to these that it is good to surrender our soul, above all when we suffer or are afraid. And in so doing there is a great happiness and great merit." By indicating when we suffer, it gives us the opportunity to let God mold us and shape us into what he wants us to be. Is God omnibenevolent? Yes, he is, because God is good all the time. Sometimes Christians suffer because they make themselves suffer and not because God lets them suffer. Also, Christians suffer so they can get stronger in the faith and have a better relationship with God.

Suffering proves how strong a Christian's faith is in God, and suffering reveals who God is. Suffering gives Christians spiritual growth if they respond properly. Sometimes God allows the suffering because it provides an opportunity for character-building, for expansion of spiritual dimension. 2 Corinthians 12:9 says, "And he said unto me, 'My grace is sufficient for thee: for my strength is made perfect in your weakness. Most gladly therefore will I rather glory in my infirmities, that the power of Christ may rest upon me.'" Christians suffer because Christ suffered, also because they want to walk, talk, and be like Him. Romans 8:17 says; "And if children, then heirs; heirs of God, and joint heirs with Christ; if so be that we suffer with him, that we may be also glorified together."

Gustavo Gutierrez says to be a believer means sharing human suffering—especially that of the most destitute—enduring a spiritual struggle, and, finally, accepting the fact that God cannot be pigeon-holed into human categories. In Job, there is the question of telling the innocent who are beset by unjust suffering that God loves them—and that their legitimate demand for justice for themselves and others acquires it's fullest measure and greatest urgency in the universe of gratuitousness (p. 16).

In his suffering Job wanted God to know that he knew that God is "I am that I am." Job writes these words in Job 6:2-3, 8-10; "Oh that my grief were thoroughly weighed, and my calamity laid in the balances together. For now it would be heavier than the sand of the sea: therefore my words are swallowed up. Oh that I might have my request; and that God would grant me the things that I long for! even that it would please God to destroy me; that he would let loose his hand, and cut me off! Then should I yet have comfort; yea, I would harden myself in sorrow: let him not spare; for I have not concealed the works of the Holy One."

It is revealed by studying these scriptures that Job wanted God to let him know when he did anything displeasing or ungodly. He wanted God to take him because he did not want to bear false witness against God, and his friends told Job that he had barely sinned. False witness means sinning against God. Gustavo Gutierrez stated, "Job expresses his exultation with a certain pride: he has not blasphemed. Nonetheless he sees that his words of complaint may have gone beyond what he intended. But in the midst of his sufferings, he has no other way of expressing himself, and therefore he pleads to be heard and given an answer." He feels more alone than ever. The discussion begun with his friends quickly turned into a dialogue of the deaf. The doctrine these theologians profess does not allow them to hear what others are saying; the echo of their own words stops up their ears. Job says to them, "Will no one teach you to be quiet the only wisdom that become you! Kindly listen to my accusation and your attention to the way I shall plead." (Job 38-41)

The interesting part about Job's suffering is that Job's friends convinced themselves he had sinned against God, but Job didn't suffer because he had sinned. Job suffered because God wanted him to become wise.

Shakespeare's *King Lear* suggests that spiritual suffering is more intense than physical suffering, that spiritual suffering may be a consequence of moral end, and that spiritual suffering can be transformed from an evil to a good. It's impossible to review the whole range and variety of human suffering, but the facts must be faced honestly, without accepting a dualism of nature and God. (p. 15) Individual reaction to the fact is of the first importance, and pain may be our path to the first real discovery of God. The problem becomes practical and acute in the individual experience. But before the reality of divine providence is denied, people should recognize that a personal relation to God lifts the problem to a new level on which there is a new standard of values and the operation of a larger purpose. On this level, there is a transvaluation of suffering, but a great residual problem remains. Christians' only hope of facing this successfully is by appealing to the love of God, who does not shrink from suffering, in us, and with us, and for us.

Another point that supports this perspective is about the claim that God suffers. It rests on the Biblical revelation of him and particularly on the fact of the suffering of Jesus Christ. The Greek theology of the early church, however, on philosophical grounds, rejected any ascription of suffering to God. Modern theology has returned to the assertion of divine possibility, but there are serious philosophical objections that must be faced; in other words, that divine possibility implies 1) frustration, 2) entanglement in the time process, 3) the conception of a God less than the absolute of philosophy. (*Suffering and Divine*, p. 19) These objections can be met, for; Self-limitation is not frustration, God is not in time, but time is in God (p. 18) and the concept of the absolute must not be that of God and the Father and of Jesus Christ, continuously active in creation and redemption. Has God's love any meaning if it is not costly to Him, as well as to Jesus? Both the suffering of the Son and the suffering of the Holy Spirit reveal and imply a suffering Father. *(Suffering and Divine,* p. 19)

The fellowship of God with man that has its earthly center at the cross has two great applications to the residual problem of unexplained human suffering. Man can firmly trust God because of his actualized "sympathy," and man is invited to share in the fellowship of Christ's sufferings, by which evil is transformed to good. Thus the redemptive work of Christ is continued in all who are his, and the eternal reality is continually being actualized in the temporal world. (*Suffering and Divine,* p. 19)

Suffering must be interpreted from within the creative fellowship of God through Christ. This enables the believer to welcome even suffering as a divinely given opportunity. Through suffering, Christians learn both humility and sympathy with others, and they have the opportunity to give effective witness to their faith. Fellowship with Jesus implies "cross bearing" with him. The conditions of such a *Solvitur Patiendo* as H. Wheeler Robinson defines; a persistent purpose, a reference to something beyond the suffering, and the winning of peace through suffering and not the evasion of it. These conditions are how H. Wheeler Robinson defines suffering to a human being when it comes to his relationship with God, and to us as Christians.

The following is a script from Rufus Jones, who helped establish the American French Service Commission in 1917, that he edited from Dr. Robinson's theory on human suffering: "What suffering, physical, mental and spiritual, is rampant in this world is an inescapable fact. Man has always displayed an amazing capacity to endure physical pain, and with the advance of science much has been done to ease its ravages. But it is mental and spiritual suffering which takes the far greater toll in broken lives, and this toll is rising with the march of years in our turbulent civilization beset with social, political and economic distress." This mental and spiritual cross exists in the life of every man. Is it to be merely a growing, distressing end, or can it be transformed into a good, not only for individuals but for the human race and for God? There is positive value in facing the harsh realities of life and the inevitableness of nature. Hardship, not ease, tempers the characters and souls of men; it is the spirit which they display during their ordeal which determines whether it makes them or breaks them. It is with this crucial spiritual factor that Dr. Robinson deals. He demonstrates that suffering must be interpreted from within a creative fellowship with Christ. The fellowship implies "cross-bearing" with him. Ultimate and lasting peace and happiness are won through suffering, not enduring it. When it comes to suffering, again, man tries to think like God. In Isaiah 55:89, God says, "For my thoughts are not your thoughts, neither are your ways my ways, saith the Lord. For as the heavens are higher than the earth, so are my ways higher than your ways, and my thoughts than your thoughts." What the scripture is saying is that a person might want a Jaguar, but the Lord might want them to have a Pinto. Both are cars, but the Pinto is not a luxury car like the Jaguar; though the Pinto can get to a destination just like the Jaguar. In other words, what a person might want might not be what they need.

The story of the cross is very relevant to the whole problem of suffering. Christ didn't passively endure it while God looked on. He took such an attitude to it, accepting it in such a positive and trusting spirit, that he wrestled from it. He met the evil that man did to him as one might rectify the debit account in a ledger with a credit, so that Good Friday wasn't a sad story with a happy ending on Easter Day. Both are days of triumph.

Good Friday was terrible for Jesus, beyond our power to comprehend. The cross felt like defeat, it looked like defeat, and it was called defeat. It seemed as if evil had triumphed, and his cause was lost. He felt deserted even by his Father, but that suffering, which wouldn't run away, revealed itself to be the greatest redemptive force the world has ever known. H.H. Farmer, who was a theologian at the University of Cambridge, once pointed out, "You cannot defeat." Men could only "look on him whom they had pierced" and break down at the wonder and grandeur and power of such a revelation of the nature of God. (p. 19 and 20 of *Salute To a Sufferer*) Not in spite of the cross but through the cross, the ultimate aim of God in Christ was achieved as completely as it would have been had men followed Christ from the beginning instead of murdering him. That is why Christians place the cross in the very center of what they call God's plan of redemption.

So, in the case of human suffering, God doesn't will it or desire it, but it won't defeat him in his plan for the individual sufferer; and he has such a plan for each individual. The fact that the suffering is allowed at all carries the guarantee that God, so far from being defeated by it finally can weave it into a pattern as wonderful as one which left out suffering completely. God can bring humans—not in spite of their suffering, but because of it and his use of it and humans' reaction to it—to the same place as they should have reached if suffering had never come our way. Humans will earn final gain instead of loss. When it comes to suffering, unbearable and intolerable as Christians often feel suffering to be, it's a sign that God cares enough. Wouldn't it be much, much easier if he either blotted humans out altogether or was content to use his power merely to achieve humans' happiness instead of bothering with individual characters? The gold refiner goes on using fire until he can see his own image reflected in the gold. God does the same with men, using the fire he didn't make to serve his purpose. (1 Cor. 3:12-15, 1 Pet. 1:7)

Another factor that must be examined when it comes to suffering is this: "But the God who left us alone as we are now would not be God." God will use any means, including the suffering he doesn't will, to shape humans and alter them and improve them and win them from their wild, filthy, foul, and unclean habits, so that at last they may be made ready to enter into a communion with Him, the depths of which have never been plumbed. (*Salute To A Sufferer*, p. 27)

When the Apostle Paul talks about suffering he says, "Our light affliction, which is but for a moment, worketh for us a far more exceeding and eternal weight of glory; while we look not at the things which are seen, but at the things which are not seen: for the things which are seen are temporal; but the things which are not seen are eternal." (21 Cor. 4:17-18) "Happiness is a truth. It's always a by-product development contributes to the glory of god which is the end of all human existence." (*Salute To A Sufferer*, p. 38 & 29) The Apostle Paul talks about suffering; one can suffer because one might put all their trust and faith in material objects. Paul says look toward heaven and the greater gifts that God will give you. Earthly materials are here only for a little while, but God's gift will last forever.

The conquest of suffering is what is really meant by the conquest of nature, thus suffering is what is really meant by the conquest of nature. Suffering becomes, for modern times, what it never was for any pre-modern civilizations. The greatest problem there is that the thing that must be overcome is the greater evil of sin seen in terms of the lesser end of suffering. The only sin the modern mind really feels strongly about is cruelty. Modern people find it very hard to comprehend the Biblical (and universal) myth of paradise lost, where suffering and death are seen in terms of sin rather than vice versa. The Christian story, therefore, also seems incomplete and a failure to the modern mind. Christ conquered sin, but he didn't yet abolish the need for us to suffer and die. A God who didn't abolish suffering—worse, a God who abolished sin precisely by suffering—is a scandal to the modern mind, for to that mind such a solution seems to ignore the primary problem. To Christian minds, it is modernity which ignores the primary problem.

In short, if the most important thing in life is reconciliation with God, union with God, conformity to God, then any price is worth paying to obtain that end. If the most important thing in life is conquering suffering and attaining pleasure—comfort and power by man's conquest of nature—then Jesus is a fool and a failure. (*Making Sense Out of Suffering*, p. 29-30) Christians know that Jesus is no fool but man is. Christ's work won for man a world free of suffering, free of sin; a world called heaven, or God's house, God's family mansion. Man is presently beginning preparation, purification, or purgatory, the training. Men are only spiritual babies, and man is learning of the elementary ways of that house, and learning very slowly. Christians have to take many scalding hot baths, a painful process to wash the dirt off, but the process is already part of the mansion (heaven). If men are in Christ, then men are already in paradise; "God allows the suffering because he wants the human family to learn, to substitute knowledge for its ignorance, wisdom for its folly and holiness for its sin; and these three exchanges cannot be imposed on human nature. They have to be achieved by the hard way of learning. (*Salute To A Sufferer*, p. 17)

One can examine this topic over and over but still come up with the same answer; suffering strengthens the mind, the body, and most importantly, the spiritual nature of a Christian. Some might say that suffering is part of the price the team pays in its great struggle toward perfection and being a Christian; suffering in humans' strive toward perfection, and that is like being with Christ.

In conclusion, one must understand Christians suffer so we can be molded and shaped toward God's will. It isn't to hurt, but to make stronger and wiser.

Understand what is required by Christians if they are to be like Christ. Pray with the knowledge of faith, knowing that the heavenly Father will answer our prayers. Fast for the strength to overcome our obstacles, and have the faith that all these things work together for the good. Also, know the word of God that it might enlighten those who are in darkness, that they may come to know Jesus as their personal savior. By studying they can approach those who think they're walking in the light with sound doctrine. How do Christians know when they have the right leader in the right position; by those who speak of the true gospel, the death, burial, and resurrection of Jesus Christ. Earthly materials—don't lay a heart upon them, there are greater rewards in heaven.

Hopefully, one has come to a better understanding of how to function in a dysfunctional society. Always remember that without God being the head of a Christian's life, that Christian will always be in a dysfunctional situation.

How does a Christian function in a dysfunctional society?

This book seeks to better equip Christians to make productive choices regarding personal development in the areas of prayer, fasting, and faith. Developing stronger studying techniques also will make the reader aware of different obstructs that will fall into their path.

This book also shows the level of commitment a Christian must take in order to be an effective Christian in today's society. It also shows how the Bible is the true word of God and how to use it against untrue statements, false teachers and preachers, and the many different cults that face us today. For Christians, when it comes to the Word of God and dealing with all these different religions in this dysfunctional society, the answer is: Seek God first, study His Word, and go out and tell those who do not know, and have Jesus Christ as their personal Savior—Jesus is the answer for the world today. The true religion is the Gospel of Jesus Christ. No Vedas, no Buddha, no Guru Maharaja, no Moon, no Mary Bakker Eddy, no Joseph Smith, no Charles Russel. These people and statues are not gods nor masters. The true religion is the death, burial, and resurrection of Jesus Christ.

BIBLIOGRAPHY

Altman, Alexander. 1981. Essays *In Jewish Intellectual History.* University Press of New England/

Anderson, James D. and Egia Earl Jones. 1978. *The Management of Ministry, Leadership, Purpose.* Harper and Row Publishers.

Anthony, Michael J. 1993. *Effective Church Boards.* Baker Books.

Armstrong, Herbert W. 1981. *The Missing Dimension In Sex.* Pickering, Ontario: Beaver Books.

Arnheim, Michael. 1984. *Is Christianity True?* Prometheus.

Applegarth, Margaret T. 1957. *Twelve Baskets Full.* Harper and Brothers Publishers.

Betts, Robert Brenton. 1975. *Christians In The Arab East.* John Knox Press.

Boring, M. Eugene. 1989. *Opposition to Paul in Jewish Christianity.* Fortress Press.

Bowker, John. 1970. *The Problems of Suffering in Religions of the World.* Cambridge University Press.

Brooke, Rosalind, and Christopher Brooke. 1984. *Popular Religion in the Middle Ages: Western Europe 1000-1300.* Thames and Hudson.

Brooks, Keith L., comp. 1976. *The Spirit of Truth and the Spirit of Error: What God Has Said on Seven Fundamentals and What Men Are Now Saying.* Revised by Irvine Robertson. Moody Press.

Butterworth, John. 1981. *A Book of Beliefs, Cults and New Faiths.* David C. Cook Publishing Co.

Buttrich, George Arthur. 1941. *Prayer.* Abington Cokesbury Press.

Carpenter, B. D., Rev. S. C. 1919. *Christianity According to Saint Luke.* The Macmillan Company.

Carrel, Dr. Alexis. 1947. *Prayer.* Hodder and Stoughton.

Carretto, Carol. 1986. *Why, O Lord?: The Inner Meaning Of Suffering.* Maryknoll, NY: Orbis Books.

Cerminaia, Gina. 1950. *Many Mansions.* New American Library.

Clebsch, William A. 1979. *Christianity In European History.* New York: Oxford University Press.

Coote, Robert B. and Mary P. Coote. 1990. *Power, Politics and the Making of the Bible.* Fortress Press.

Cotham, Perry C. 1976. *Politics, Americanism and Christianity.* Baker Book House.

Crane, Jim. 1969. *A Funny Thing Happened On The Way To Heaven.* Harper and Row Publishers.

de Chardin, Pierre Terlhard. *On Suffering.* Harper and Row.

Dingman, Robert W. 1989. *The Complete Search Committee Guide Book.* Regal Books.

Douty, Mary Alice. 1957. *How To Work With Church Groups.* Abington Press.

Dreyfus, Hippolyte. 1957. *The Universal Religion: Bahaism.* Cope and Fenwich.

Dudley, Carl S. 1979. *Where Have All Our People Gone?* The Pilgrim Press.

Ellul, Jacques. 1970. *Prayer and Modern Man.* Seabury Press.

Falwell, Jerry. 1984. *When It Hurts Too Much To Cry.* Tyndale House Publishers, Inc.

Faulring, Scott H., ed. 1989. *An American Prophet's Record: The Dairies and Journals of Joseph Smith.* Signature Books, Inc.

Forem, Jack. 1943. *Transcendental Meditation, Maharishi Mahesh Yogi and the Science of Creative Intelligence.* New York: Dutton.

Forsyth, P. T. 1916. *The Souls Of Prayer.* Grand Rapids, MI: William B. Eerdmans Publishing Co.

Fosdick, Harry Emerson. 1917. *The Meaning Of Faith.* International Committee of the Young Men's Christian Association.

Fowler, Henry Thatcher. 1916. *Origin and Growth of the Hebrew Religion.* Chicago: The University of Chicago Press.

Gilmore, G. Don. 1982. *No Matter How Dark The Valley: The Power of Faith in Times of Need.* San Francisco: Harper and Row.

Gleber, S. Michael. 1975. *Job, Stand Up.* New York: The Union of American Hebrew Congregation.

Godin, S. J. 1935. *Prayer and the Bible.* Fleming H. Revell Company.

Grenfell, M. D., Wilfred T. and Sidney A. Weston. 1926. *A Man's Faith.* The Jordan and More Press.

Grith, James L. and John C. Green, eds. *The Bible and the Ballot Box: Religion and Politics in the 1988 Election.* Westview Press.

Gutierrez, Gustano. 1987. *On Job and God: Talk and Suffering of the Innocent.* Maryknoll, NY: Orbis Books.

Harkness, Georgia. 1952. *Disciplines of the Christian Life.* John Knox Press.

Hebblethearte, Brian. 1976. *Evil, Suffering and Religion.* New York: Hawthorn Books, Inc.

Heller, Friedrich. 1932. *Prayer: A Study in the History and Psychology of Religion.* Oxford University Press.

Howard, M.A., D.D., W.F. 1946. *Christianity According to Saint John.* The Westminster Press.

Howlett, Duncan. 1957. *The Essence and Christianity.* New York: Harper and Brothers.

Hymes, Jr., James L. 1949. *Discipline.* New York:

Bureau Of Publications Teachers College, Columbia University.

Jackson, Elizabeth. 1944. *The Faith and Fire Within Us.* The University of Minnesota Press.

Johnson, James Turner, ed. 1985. *The Bible In American Law: Politics and Political Rhetoric.* Fortress Press.

Jones, Rufus Matthew. 1938. *Great Issues Of Life.* The Macmillan Company.

Kautsky, Karl. 1953. Translated by Henry F. Mins. *Foundations of Christianity.* Library of Congress.

Kreeft, Peter. 1986. *Making Sense Out Of Suffering.* Ann Arbor, MI: Servant Books.

Laymen, Richard. 1990. *Volume 1: Child Abuse.* Omnigraphics.

Liderbeck, Daniel. 1992. *Why Do We Suffer?: New Ways Of Understanding.* Paulist Press.

Mann, Gerald. 1992. *When The Bad Times Are Over For Good: Transforming Trouble Into Triumph.* New York: McCracken Press.

McCabe, Joseph. 1920. *Spiritualism.* Dodd, Meade and Company.

McIntire, C. T. 1977. God, *History and Historians: An Anthology of Modern Christian Views of History.* Oxford University Press.

McNeill, John Thomas, Matthew Spinka and Harold R. Willoughby, eds. 1939. *Environmental Factors In Christian History.* Kennikat Press.

Moot, M. A., John R. 19081. *The Future Leadership of the Church.* Student Department, Young Christian Assoc.

Munzy, David Saville, Emma Peters Smith, Ernest Bahaut and James T. Shotwell. 1929. *Essay In Intellectual History.* AMS Press.

Myers, Edward P. 1978. *The Problem of Evil and Suffering.* Howard Ruhleaher.

Neibuhr, Richard. 1956. *The Purpose of the Church and Its Ministry.* New York: Harper and Brothers.

Patterson, Dolly K., ed. 1980. *Questions of Faith: Contemporary Thinkers Respond.* Trinity Press International.

Paul, Robert S. 1972. *The Church In Search Of Itself.*
William B. Eerchmans Publishing Co.

Peters, F. E. 1990. *Judiasm, Christianity and Islam.*
Princeton University Press.

Rahner, S. J., Hugo. 1971. *Greek Myths and Christian
Mystery.* New York: Bible and Tannen.

Ramsey, Paul. 1957. *Faith and Ethics: The Theology of
Nieburh.* Harper and Row Publishers.

Reinhardt, Kurt F., 1960. *The Agony of Christianity.*
Frederich Ungar Publishing Co.

Robinson, M.A., D.D., H. Wheeler. 1939. *Suffering,
Human and Divine.* The Macmillan Company.

----------------------. 1955. *The Cross In The Old Testament.* The Westminster Press.

Ross, Shirley. 1976. *Fasting.* St. Martin's Press.

Roth, Leon. 1960. *Judiasm, A Portrait.* New York: The
Viking Press.

Sanford, John A. 1993. *Mystical Christianity: A Psy-
chological Commentary on the Gospel of John.* The
Crossroad Publishing Company.

Schaller, Lyle E. 1973. *The Pastor and the People.* Abington Press.

Schillbeeker, Edward. 1981. *Ministry Leadership in the Community of Jesus Christ.* The Crossroad Publishing Company.

Schweitzer, Albert. 1967. *The Kingdom of God and Primitive Christianity.* The Seabury Press.

Shoemaker, Samuel M. 1963. *Beginning Your Ministry.* Harper and Row Publishers.

Silberger, M. D., Julius. 1980. *Mary Baker Eddy: An Interpretive Biography of the Founder of Christian Science.* Little, Brown and Company.

Silner, Abba Hillel. 1956. *Where Judaism Differed.* The Macmillan Company.

Slattery, D. D., Charles Lewis. 1921. *The Ministry.* Charles Scribner & Sons.

Smith, Lucy. 1969. *Biographical Sketches of Joseph Smith, The Prophet.* Arno Press and The New York Times.

Sontag, Frederich. 1970. *God, Why Did You Do That?.* Westminster Press.

Spear, Wayne R. 1979. *The Theology of Prayer: A Systematic Study of the Biblical Teaching on Prayer.* Grand Rapids, MI: Baker Book House.

Stein, Murray. 1985. *Jung's Treatment of Christianity: The Psychotherapy of a Religious Tradition.* Chiron Publications.

Steinberg, Milton. 1951. *A Believing Jew.* New York: Harcourt, Brace and Co.

Tatelbaum, Judy. 1989. *You Don't Have To Suffer.* New York: Harper and Row Publishers.

Toynbee, Arnold. 1957. *Christianity Among Religions of the World.* New York: Charles Scribner's & Sons.

Weatherhead, Leslie D. 1962. *Salute To A Sufferer.* New York and Nashville, TN: Abington Press.

--------------------. 1936. *Why Do Men Suffer?* The Abington Press.

Weber, Max. 1952. Translated and edited by Hans H. Gerth and Don Martindale. *Ancient Judaism.* Glencoe, IL: The Free Press.

Woods, Bobby W. 1974. *Understanding Suffering.* Baker Book House.